A PAST

A Past with a Future

JIM GRAHAM

KINGSWAY PUBLICATIONS
EASTBOURNE

First published 1987

ISBN 0 86065 418 4

Front cover design by Vic Mitchell

Printed in Great Britain for
KINGSWAY PUBLICATIONS LTD
Lottbridge Drove, Eastbourne, E. Sussex BN23 6NT by
Richard Clay Ltd, Bungay, Suffolk.
Typeset by CST, Eastbourne, E. Sussex.

Contents

To Nicholas and Leslie, David, John and Andrew —
my family, who represent a new generation,
and whose lives challenge me and society
with their honesty and faith.

Acknowledgements

I am so grateful to Pam Kerr, who has so willingly typed the manuscript for this book and with care and enthusiasm corrected it. My thanks are also due to my secretary, Shirley Rothwell, who with very great patience helps me with my writing, among many other activities. I am thankful, too, to the team here at the church of which I am a part for their loyalty and understanding in a programme which generates considerable pressure.

As ever I am grateful to Anne — my wife, my best friend and my constant supporter — for being herself, and thereby ministering the life of Jesus to me in so many ways.

1

A Vision and a Voice

A friend of mine was attending a Rotary lunch at which a number of people were arguing over which was the longest established business in the community. Eventually the local vicar, having listened to everyone else, stood up and declared, 'My "business" is the longest established in the community!' He was right, of course. But there lies the strength and weakness of the church. There is dignity and security in longevity, but often there is also irrelevance and weakness. Perhaps an even greater hindrance to the church than her roots in antiquity are the anachronisms which continue to be part of her contemporary life. Her Norman architecture, Roman dress and Victorian language hardly commend her to a world of space exploration, supersonic speed, computerized technology and 'star wars' defence programmes.

The fact of the matter is, however, that a new day is dawning for the church in the latter part of the twentieth century. Christians of my own denominational background gave little attention to the church as such. 'We want Christianity, not Churchianity!' was the slogan I often heard repeated in the circles in which I was reared. Evangelicals were very interested in the gospel of Jesus (interested, but not all that excited by it!) but were largely uninterested in the church which Jesus left behind. Now we are becoming aware once more that the past has a future and that in order to secure that future we need to go back to the past. We need to go back to the beginnings of the church if hope and direction are to beckon us into the days ahead.

The difference between the gospel of Luke and the Acts of the Apostles is that Jesus changed bodies. In Luke we see him in his incarnate body, in God-made flesh, sharing our humanity, aware of the pressures under which we live and the problems to which we do not always find solutions. Then Jesus died, rose again and ascended to the place of authority with his Father. Now there is a man in heaven—for Jesus did not bear our humanity for thirty-three years, but for eternity.

So after the ascension God needed a new body on earth to declare his word and to manifest his power. That new body began to function dynamically on the day of Pentecost, and we call it the church. It is into this body that God has called us as Christians. There is no such thing as solitary religion in the Bible, nor are there unattached Christians in the New Testament. It is part of the biblical understanding of conversion that we not only realize we are sinners in God's sight and repent of our sin and receive Christ as our Lord and Saviour, but having been released from the bondages put upon us by the kingdom of darkness and been baptized in water and in the Holy Spirit we become living members of the new body of Christ on earth—the church! This is conversion in the biblical sense of the word. How God needs to release us from the dull, lack-lustre, formal, monotonous mediocrity which has masqueraded as normal New Testament Christianity! Often this has been caused by a limited view of conversion, so that many of us have been badly born spiritually.

Jesus' incarnate ministry was initiated by a dramatic baptism by John the Baptist in the Jordan River in front of the multitudes. John did not spend much at the supermarket check-out, nor did he have much in the way of clothes, but he could preach, and he knew what God was like and what God wanted. Somewhat uncertain of his role, he did baptize Jesus—and then it began to happen! Jesus saw a vision and heard a voice. The vision was of the Spirit, the voice was unmistakably that of God the Father. The vision gave Jesus power, for before then there was neither miracle nor ministry in his life. The voice gave him perspective, reminding him that he was royalty (cf. Ps 2:7) and that his kingly power would be demonstrated in being a servant (cf. Is 42:1). All this happened when he was baptized and was praying.

The new body of Christ on earth—the church—was born in a similar climate. The followers of Jesus had been involved in a ten-day prayer meeting when the Spirit came upon them. No doubt these were the days when God gave them perspective about who they were, and what he wanted them to do. And then 'when the day of Pentecost came, all the believers were gathered together in one place. Suddenly . . .' it all happened! (Acts 2:1). The golden age of the church had begun, and within a generation the gospel of Jesus Christ had exploded from the religious capital of the world, Jerusalem, and had penetrated the political capital of the world, Rome—and beyond. A numerical, social, cultural and geographical miracle walked before men in the arena of human history—the new body of Christ on earth, the church.

This was the church as God intended it to be. Often our problem is not that we are too traditional, but that we are not traditional enough. We limit our tradition to a specific time in history rather than push right back into New Testament times when the church was 'vigorous and flexible, for these are the days before it ever became fat and short of breath through prosperity, or muscle-bound by over-organization'.[1] We need again to see a vision, that heaven is still open and the Holy Spirit still wants to descend on God's people in power; we need to hear a voice, the voice of God reminding us who we are and what he wants us to do.

I first made the acquaintance with the thinking and writing of the philosopher Soren Kierkegaard when I was up at Glasgow University reading Philosophy. His thinking is very stimulating, but never was it more shrewd than when he observed, 'Whereas Christ turned water into wine, the Church has succeeded in doing something more difficult; it has turned wine into water.' The interest in Jesus today is unmistakeable. Books, plays, discussions and musicals bear eloquent testimony to that, but the church has been given the thumbs-down in our western culture. To most people the church means empty, old-fashioned, decaying buildings, elderly and predominately female congregations and a depressed, disaffected and bewildered clergy.It is regarded at best as an irrelevance and at worst as a running sore within society that needs to be removed. 'Nothing in the contemporary scene is more striking,' writes Bishop Stephen Neill, 'than the general regard which is felt for Jesus Christ and the general dislike of the organised church which bears His Name.'[2]

The United Kingdom has a Christian heritage which is second to none. We have been preserved from invasion by an enemy for the last thousand years. We, as a nation, received the gospel of Jesus Christ within about thirty years of his death and resurrection, since the first Christian martyr in Britain was Albanus, a Roman soldier of the occupying forces of that time.

The town of St Albans bears his name and preserves his memory. Over 90% of the British population still live within walking distance of a church building or a Christian meeting place. In a society where the doctor has become the priest, there are still more clergy per head of the population than there are medical practitioners. We have more translations and paraphrases of the Bible in English than we know what to do with. As I look round the shelves of my own office I can count fifteen different translations. Over the past quarter of a century God has been pouring out his Spirit again upon his people in this country. It all adds up to a nation enormously privileged by God.

And yet even in his day, William Temple could speak of 'the vast chaos which for us represents the church, with its hateful cleavages, its slow-moving machinery, its pedantic antiquarianism . . . its indifference to much that is fundamental, its age-long ineffectiveness, its abundant capacity for taking the wrong side on moral issues.'

So the church's fumbling ineptitude is not a new thing. An article in the *Weekend Telegraph* has commented:

> England has been officially Christian for more than fifteen hundred years. Our whole culture is based on Christianity. However, today it is apparently no longer respectable, or even acceptable actually to *be* a Christian. This is especially so among people of my own age and type. Humanism is the thing. It is not that religion in general is out. Roman Catholics are all right because one is generally born a Roman Catholic and so cannot do anything about it. Mormons are O.K. too—not to be one, but for sociological study purposes. The Eastern religions are very trendy. But as for ordinary God-fearing Bible-reading, Christ-imitating Christianity—it's plain old-fashioned. You're barmy, a freak, if you believe in it these days.

In spite of the fact that King Alfred wrote the Ten Commandments at the top of our English constitutional laws, the one thing which these commandments seek to preserve—respect—has gone from our nation. The notice, *Shoplifters will be prosecuted,* is a common sight in our shops. Respect for property has all but gone.

Mass abortion, the apparently unrestrained experimentation on the human embryo and the inception of 'Exit' to facilitate euthanasia clearly herald the disappearance of another bulwark of our society—respect for life.

The Matrimonial and Family Proceedings Act (1984) ensured the possible destruction of a marriage within one year, providing both partners agree. This was another stage in the erosion of a fundamental institution of our society. We are witnessing an alarming decline in respect for marriage.

How important it is to us to recall the Russian dissident Alexander Solzhenitsyn's conclusion on BBC's *Panorama* in March 1976: 'I wouldn't be surprised at the sudden and imminent fall of the West . . . Nuclear war is not even necessary to the Soviet Union. You can be taken simply with bare hands.' Here in the West we are in sharp decline. We are too flabby and lethargic to do anything about our crumbling civilization or to do battle with the strong, marauding forces of Marxism, Islam and Humanism. According to the exhaustive study at the Centre for World Evangelisation in Nairobi in 1979 (as a result of analysing statistics from the world's 223 countries, its 6,270 ethno-linguistic groups, its fifty major religions and more than 9,000 Christian denominations), 1,815,100 adult professing Christians in Europe abandoned the faith to become agnostics, atheists or adherents of non-Christian religions or cults. North America registered a decline of 950,000. All these were net figures, after conversions to Christianity had been noted. During the same period, however, churches in the Third World experienced extraordinary gains. In Africa the net gain was 6,152,800—that's 16,000 a day! In South Asia the number converted was 34,813,000.

Considered globally, the church is certainly not a relic of the past. It is growing more rapidly today than at any other period in its history. In 1900 7½% of the population of Africa was Christian; today the percentage is 33% and expected to rise to 50% by AD 2000. In Latin America the current growth of population is 3%; yet among evangelical Christians alone the growth rate in recent years has been 10%. There are some seventy million Christians in Asia. In the vast country of Indonesia, there have been over 50,000 baptisms in five years. In the Third World more than 200 missionary societies have been founded in the last few years, with 3,000 missionaries sent out. So Christianity cannot be dismissed as a last-ditch stand of middle-class culture in the West. It is confidently declared that there are 1,300 million Christians in the world—over 30% of the total population of this planet, and more than double that of any of the other great world religions.

The development and persistence of the church is incredible and beyond our ability to understand apart from the reality of the grace and purposes of God. In the first 300 years of her life she underwent the most vicious and unbelievable persecution under the hands of a succession of Roman Emperors—Nero, Domitian, Trajan, Marcus Aurelius, Decius and Diocletian. This continued until the time of Constantine, who had ensured that Christianity would be the only state religion. It proved in hindsight to be a mixed blessing, as the hierarchical structure of bishops and priests hardened and became inflexible and a widening gap emerged between the ordained clergy and the laymen who comprised the church. Formal liturgical worship was emphasized to such an extent that the life-giving power of the Holy Spirit was no longer able to flow. As the political power of the Roman Empire declined through moral decay from within and the military devastation by the barbarian hosts from without, the now institutional church based on Rome, devoid of real spiritual vitality, grew enormously in financial stature and structural strength and so became the dominating force in the Middle Ages. With the gathering strength of the Eastern Churches under the leadership of the Patriarch in Constantinople a division was inevitable and two centres of Christianity eventually emerged—one in the West, Rome; and the other in the East, Constantinople.

Powerful emperors quickly saw the strategic political potential of the church and so seized control not only of the state, but also of the church. This led quickly and disastrously to five centuries of spiritual decline and the effective stagnation of the church. Sadness was built upon sadness, and by the tenth century the Papacy had reached an all-time low. There was only one way the church could now go—upwards! No other direction was open to it.

In the midst of the dark, seemingly impenetrable clouds which enshrouded her life there remained shafts of light. For example, as far back as the sixth century spiritual life continued to flow through monastic renewal initiated by Benedict. This was encouraged by the spiritual and moral reforms of Pope Gregory (1077-1088). It was continued by the now well-known Cistercians in the twelfth century and the Franciscans and the Dominicans in the thirteenth. Francis of Assissi motivated a real missionary zeal, especially directed towards the Muslims.

By the twelfth century, however, the indomitable Spirit of God which had invaded and captured the heart of man created a strong anti-clerical feeling. Although severely persecuted, the Waldensians in Italy strongly challenged the worldliness of the church and found a ready response in those who were disenchanted by the temporal power and riches of the institutional church. This created a spiritual climate in which there was a positive searching for true spirituality through the channels of both monasticism and mysticism.

Also men like Peter Abelard (1079-1142) and Thomas Aquinas (1224-1274) emerged to explore creative theological thinking. Yet again spiritual decline followed through the fourteenth and fifteenth centuries through a barren scholasticism. And so the church lost its way in the artistic pursuits of the early Renaissance.

It was in this climate that the Reformation was born. The immediate cause was the opposition to distasteful, misleading and unholy practices. For example, Indulgences were sold to secure funds for the rebuilding of St Peter's in Rome, and a glimpse of Frederick the Wise's sacred relics ensured escape from two million years in purgatory! This led to the greatest rupture in the church's history—the break from Rome. The main architects of the Protestant Reformation were Martin Luther and John Calvin. These were, however, only the 'front' men. There were masses of others, both scholarly and illiterate, who created the spiritual groundswell which shook Christendom to its foundations. This led, of course, to the Lutheran, Presbyterian and Reformed Churches being formed and to the entry onto the scene of the Puritans in England.

Both the Reformation and the Counter-Reformation which followed caused intense suffering with many martyrdoms and a legacy of bitterness and conflict. The bewildering persistence of sectarianism and blood-letting in Ireland today (four hundred years after the event!) is only one expression of this. However, there were some very positive and creative results which brought life, hope and the resurgence of spiritual power and relevance. Biblical doctrines were rediscovered and the church was reformed as a result.

Yet even among the reformers there were conflict and controversy. The Anabaptists, for example, felt that Luther and Calvin had not gone far enough, and they rejected the idea of a national or territorial church, and powerfully taught the concept of the 'gathered fellowship'—the coming together of only committed Christians with a personal faith and testimony to Jesus Christ as Lord and Saviour—and baptized only those who were believers.

Protestant Zurich acted strongly against independent baptism outside the control of the organized church. Anyone attending an Anabaptist service was liable to be drowned by the ecclesiastical authorities. Proportionately more Anabaptists were martyred for their faith than any other Christian group in history. Many Anabaptists fled to America, and the Mennonites became their descendants there. During the seventeenth century in England the Baptists emerged and became the largest Christian group in the world apart from the Roman Catholics.

The Church of England was a significant product of the Reformation in England. King Henry VIII, about whom much has been written yet little is popularly known, broke with Rome in 1532 for political and personal reasons. This created a middle way between Roman Catholicism and Puritanism. Queen Mary—a devout Roman Catholic—tried to stem the tide as it flowed away from Rome, but the Puritans grew in strength. In the next century they led the Cromwellian revolution which attempted to overthrow the Crown. With Oliver Cromwell's death in 1658, however, the driving force died and the power of the monarchy was restored. As a result many Puritans sailed to America and had a lasting effect on the development and character of that great new nation.

Martin Luther was not the only one concerned about the decline of the Roman Church in the sixteenth century. Several popes were also troubled by the degeneracy of the church to which they belonged. As a result the Council of Trent (1542-1563) revitalized and redefined Roman Catholic doctrines and corrected abuses. A spiritual commando unit was formed—the Jesuits or the Society of Jesus—under the tutelage of Ignatius Loyola. Their role was to counter the increasing Protestant threat and engage in missionary expansion. As a result millions were added to the Roman Catholic Church in America, Africa and Asia.

At the same time persecuted Protestants—Puritans, Independents, Quakers and Baptists particularly—fled to America. They were joined later by the Lutherans and other Reformers looking for protection from the atrocities which were being committed in Europe in the name of Christ.

However, the Protestant Church lapsed into a cold, legalistic, ineffective moralism. It took men like Count Ludwig von Zinzendorf who founded the Moravian Church, with its warm missionary zeal, to stress in Europe what the Reformation had emphasized—the need for a personal experience of a living relationship with Jesus Christ and a strong appeal to the authority of the Bible. John Wesley in England (1703-1791) also challenged the established church now depressingly formal, its strength sapped by worldly comfort. As a result hundreds of thousands of ordinary people turned to Christ. This had profound social and political implications.

Many stayed within Anglicanism, bringing new life into dead structures. Others, however, felt compelled into the new denominations like the Baptists and the Congregationalists. Wesley himself, who travelled five thousand miles a year on horseback, gathered his new converts into an efficient and methodical complex of classes, each with its own leader—and so Methodism was born. Warm personal preaching for salvation and joyful hymn-singing developed through the United Kingdom and Europe and moved rapidly to America. So the great doctrines of the Christian Faith were sung as well as preached and taught, and so began a major force in Protestantism which was to continue.

Reality and life kept breaking in to the accumulating deadness and decay of the church—such is the nature of the Spirit and the heart of God. In New England in the United States, under the leadership of Jonathan Edwards (1703-1758), the first Great Awakening caught fire. It swept through the East Coast of America, and hundreds of thousands discovered reality in their relationship with Jesus Christ. The American church was revived; society was purged of corruption; and a new sense of social responsibility was developed. It was only the ferment of the American Revolution (1776) which limited the spreading spiritual fire and diverted energies in other directions. However, largely due to the influence of the Baptists and other Dissenters, the new Constitution of the United States—still acknowledged and sworn to by the elected Presidents of the United States of America—in its Bill of Rights brought about the separation of church and state. This development was a reversal of the situation which had existed ever since the conversion of Constantine fourteen centuries before.

Something comparable happened in Europe as a result of the French Revolution (1789). A sharp conflict between church and state initiated a fierce struggle well into the nineteenth century, resulting in strict laws limiting the powers of the church in France. Revolutionary turmoils were sparked off in part by what was known as the Enlightenment—an intellectual attack on the Christian faith by thinkers like Voltaire (1694-1778), who aimed at the corruption of the aristocratic French church, and Thomas Paine (1737-1809). The effect of this was to stimulate fresh theological thinking; a renewed examination of the reality and credibility of Christian claims. There was a rethinking, restating and reviving of Christianity, and so the church not only survived, but significantly moved forward.

The revivals of true religion during the eighteenth century led to an explosion of life-changing faith not seen since the first century. William Carey sailed for India in 1793, a venture of the infant Baptist Missionary Society born the previous year. The London Missionary Society made its entrance into life two years later in 1795. The missionary birth rate increased rapidly with the Netherlands Missionary Society in 1797, the Church Missionary Society in 1799, the British and Foreign Bible Society in 1804 and several missionary societies in the United States in 1810. God's river was again in spate.

The Roman Catholic Church was shaken by the revolutions of 1830 and 1848. One consequence was the Syllabus of Errors (1864) by Pope Pius IX (1846-1878), which was a strong reaction to any attack on the Church of Rome or the Papacy. It was virtually an attack on all modern religious movements. The result was that Vatican I was called in 1869, and papal infallibility in matters of faith and doctrine was decreed. These new initiatives from Rome led to a widespread revival of Catholic faith in Europe.

The Tractarian Revival or the Oxford movement sought to redress the evangelical emphasis on the Bible. Aware of the discrepancies of the Church of

Rome, some strong sacramentalists refused to accept the Ordination of Dissenters. They emphasized that the nature of the true church was to be based on ordained Anglican clergy. Whatever weaknesses and prejudices they may have had, the Tractarians restored a sense of dignity in worship and re-emphasized the importance of discipline in prayer and communion. This has had a continuing influence on Anglicanism ever since.

The Holy Spirit, however, refused to be confined to church matters, and prompted much social activism by evangelicals. People like William Wilberforce and the Clapham Sect, Lord Shaftesbury and Hannah Moore led this new development. Slavery, poor conditions in factories, child and female labour and social irresponsibility among the upper classes all became targets of spiritual assault by these campaigners.

However, the spiritual vitality which spearheaded this under the motivating love of Christ began to wane, and left a shell of hypocritical and repressive Victorian morality. Even missionary enterprise was strongly characterized by Western culture and imperialist attitudes, so that it was difficult to distinguish between the purposes of God and Western preferences and prejudices.

During the twentieth century many new challenges have had to be faced by the church. There has been an incredible *population explosion.* Just over a century and a half ago the world population was around the one thousand million mark. By 1930 that had doubled to two thousand million. Now, just over half a century later, that has doubled again to four thousand million. The implications for the church are both social and spiritual. The vast problems created by famine and hunger have to be faced in the light of the Christian gospel. Also, although the church is growing faster today than in any other time in her history, there are twice as many non-Christians now as there were at the turn of the century.

The development of *knowledge* is another significant challenge which confronts the church in the twentieth century. The micro-chip revolution has had enormous repercussions socially and economically, and expresses itself popularly in the freely and cheaply available calculator as thin as a credit card and the size of a watch. Accessibility to space through satellite and the space shuttle technology has created a new political and military climate. Sophisticated weaponry and atomic potential equivalent to more than ten tons of TNT for every man, woman and child on the face of the earth has engendered fear, insecurity and a devastating uncertainty about the future.

Parallel with this scientific and technological explosion have come intellectual attacks on the Christian faith. From the end of the last century, when the clash between Darwinism and Christianity occurred, there has been an erosion of foundational beliefs in God and the essentials of Christianity. Theological liberalism has contributed hugely to unbelief on the one hand and a harsh biblical orthodoxy devoid of compassion and practicality on the other. Dr A. W. Tozer spoke clearly about this latter phenomenon when he said: 'Everywhere among conservatives we find persons who are Bible-taught, but not Spirit-taught . . . Truth that is not experienced is no better than error, and may be fully as dangerous. The Scribes who sat in Moses' seat were not the victims of error; they were the victims of their failure to experience the truth they taught.' One way or another an air of unreality, irrelevance and confusion has settled over the message the church proclaims and the life the church lives.

The awesome reality of World War I, with its fifteen million dead, followed less than a quarter of a century later by World War II and thirty-six million dead, shattered the bright hopes and dimmed the shining eyes of man as he looked from the twentieth century towards the Utopia he had hoped to build. The real casualties were not only those who were left lying on the battlefields of the world and had their names inscribed upon the countless memorials, but those who returned soured, disillusioned, cynical and resentful to an ungrateful society.

The inter-war years saw the superficiality of the twenties being crushed and mauled by the depression of the thirties. This eroded its way into the spiritual as well as the economic life of the Western world. More than twenty years later I began my own ministry in north Glasgow and then in an industrial town in the west of Scotland and discovered a raw disenchantment and a social and economic apprehensiveness still not very far beneath the surface of many lives.

Biblical criticism and *liberal theology* alongside dispensational interpretation of the Bible stripped away the divine and supernatural elements of the gospel. As a result Christians no longer believed that God would or could do today what he had done in New Testament times. Denominational and ecumenical debates ground slowly on, making little progress and even less impact on a broken and spiritually bankrupt society. Extremists inevitably polarized so that the spiritual and social aspects of the gospel of Christ became separated, and this led to constant enmity marked by bigotry and ignorance. The net result was a virtual withdrawal of most evangelicals from the social and political scene until at least the 1960s.

During the twentieth century three major developments have had a profound impact.

1. Pentecostalism

Sauer in his *History of the Christian Church* says that Martin Luther was endowed with all the gifts of the Holy Spirit. He surely moved in the dimension of the supernatural. There is a record also of St Francis Xavier speaking languages he had never learned while on his missionary journeys. The persecuted Huguenots and the Jansenists in France later in the century certainly experienced some remarkable manifestations of the Spirit. This was not a mindless emotionalism, as some have supposed, for the brilliant philosopher Pascal was attracted to and involved with the Jansenists. If you add names like the Apostle Paul and the Roman lawyer Tertullian, you are in the league of intellectual giants and certainly not of the immature.

Some of the early Quakers 'spoke in tongues', as did one of John Wesley's best known and greatly used preachers, Thomas Walsh. On March 8th 1750 he wrote in his diary: 'This morning the Lord gave me a language I knew not of, raising my soul to Him in a wondrous manner.'

During the nineteenth century the momentum continued. Gratuitous fanaticism and excess spoiled what might have been a means of deep blessing in the church through the Irvingites (Edward Irving 1792-1834), and left a scar which has not been easy to heal. But there were very significant movements of the Holy Spirit, both in Russia and in the United States, during the nineteenth century. The impact of the well-remembered and greatly-loved ministry of D. L. Moody was not devoid of 'speaking in tongues'. Growing interest was shown in the Roman Catholic Church, until it was suppressed a little bit later in the century.

Towards the end of the nineteenth century a growing expectation of world revival bubbled up. Evidences occurred in the United States, Ireland and in other parts of Britain. The spiritual temperature was raised through the ministries of men like Moody and Sankey, and later by Torrey and Alexander. The 'Holiness Movement'—including the Methodists following John Wesley's teaching on holiness, the Salvation Army, which had just been founded, and the Keswick Convention—created a ferment in which people realized that God's power was required in order to make holiness a possibility. Yet God's power came in the New Testament not only for this purpose but also so that signs and wonders might be done in the name of Christ to validate the message of the kingdom which was being declared. By the dawning of the twentieth century spiritual awareness and expectancy was high.

It was in this climate that Pentecostalism—the fourth major strand in Christendom alongside the Orthodox Church, the Roman Catholic Church and Protestantism—was born. The influence of Pentecostalism in Latin America is enormous. As a result it is well estimated that by the beginning of the twenty-first century there will be more Christians in Latin America and Africa than in the rest of the world put together.

Pentecostalism, that important ingredient of the beating heart of New Testament Christianity, was rescued and charismatic renewal in the twentieth century has developed our awareness of it and given practical expression to it. Surely this will be recorded as one of the most significant times in the unfolding of God's purposes within human history.

On one occasion David du Plessis ('Mr Pentecost') was present at a Presbyterian Church meeting where the gifts of the Holy Spirit were manifested freely. Following the service the minister said to David, 'Do you realize—we've seen today all the gifts of the Spirit except the gift of miracles?'

'Oh yes, we have,' replied David, a courteous and gracious man, with a twinkle in his eye. 'The miracle is that all this was going on in a Presbyterian church!'

These days the same sort of thing is happening in Baptist, Anglican, Plymouth Brethren, Roman Catholic and Methodist churches. Surely Christianity is well described as 'wonder upon wonder and every wonder true!'

2. Communism

Communism has captured one third of the world this century. It was in 1917 that this ideological and political volcano erupted on an unsuspecting world. However, its origins lay much further back in the mid-nineteenth century. Marx and Engels had produced their *Manifesto of the Communist Party* in 1848, and Marx himself had released *Das Kapital* in 1867. At that time it seemed little more than a theory and concept discussed and debated by intellectuals and political gourmets. However, pressure built rapidly towards the turn of the century through the enormously increasing tension between privileged and underprivileged. Since 1917 Communism has become the fastest growing movement in modern history. It has produced the greatest mass murderer of all time too—Joseph Stalin. Consistently the church has been persecuted under Communist rule, not to mention the atrocities committed against Jews.

Although Karl Marx, as a Jew, was greatly influenced by the Old Testament prophets (so, incidentally, was Jesus Christ!), the differences between Communism and Christianity leave each poles apart. For example, Communism is based on law enforced by the state or its secret police, while Christianity is based on love stimulated and sustained by the Holy Spirit. Communism is absolutely atheistic whereas Christianity by derivation is God-honouring. Communism is based on hatred of the rich, but Christianity is based on love for the poor. The ideal of Communism is that each shall receive all according to his need, but in practice that ideal has degenerated to each shall receive according to his work. Where Christianity has properly functioned in the power of the Holy Spirit 'there was no one in the group who was in need'. Private property has never been wrenched from the hands of the individual and put into the hands of either the church or state by Christianity. Rather, it has been left in individual hands to be released freely under the direction and control of the Spirit of Jesus. Communism takes a diametrically opposite view and demands that property must not remain in private hands. Communism has seen itself as functioning universally while Christianity has been concerned to operate locally.

Although Communism has consistently persecuted the church (albeit sometimes giving a public acquiescence to its existence!), the church has not only survived, but actually flourished. In fact it has flourished more dramatically under Communism than under capitalism. In China, for example, it is estimated there were one million Christians by 1950. As we move further into the 1980s it is confidently and legitimately asserted that there are now thirty to fifty million Christians in China. The Soviet newspaper *Pravda* has had to report the persistence of religious belief despite widespread and often ghoulish efforts to convert the Russian population of 270 million to atheism.

Surely the prophetic word and spiritual axiom has been demonstrated yet again that a root is able to arise out of a dry ground, and the desert, under the hand of God, must blossom as a rose.

3. Islam

It is true that the Russians could be in Paris within forty-eight hours, yet the main threat to the church in the twentieth century is coming from a completely different source—Islam. Muslims claim 17% of the world population, totalling 700 million and mostly living in the great belt of land stretching from the Atlantic coast of North Africa to deep in Central Asia and the South Pacific. It is the majority religion in thirty-five countries.

So far as Britain is concerned, we are already in the hands of the Muslim world, because we have become financially dependent on it. If the Arabs decided to cancel their investments in London and withdraw their orders for exports, the economic fabric of the United Kingdom would be torn apart. We have become alarmingly dependent on a system which through the centuries has been Christianity's greatest and most successful opponent and until recently has been impervious to the Christian gospel.

Within recent years Islam has expanded rapidly in Britain. Mosques proliferate and Islam has become the largest non-Christian religion in the country. One of our staff only recently led a faith-sharing team in south-west London and was struck by the empty churches and the queue of people standing in the January rain waiting to get into the mosque. This is Britain as we move toward the end of the twentieth century.

However, certain spiritual strands are clear within our society. A spiritual vacuum has been created and is increasingly recognized. There is a growing awareness of the utter futility of life without God. A new hunger and thirst for spiritual reality has emerged and the old order of the established and organized church will not satisfy it. Reliance on structures and traditions instead of a vital experience of the Holy Spirit is quickly disappearing. The formularies and creeds of the church —devoid of real spiritual life—will never satisfy those who in their own different and personal ways are searching for the living God.

The church needs to rediscover its identity, originally given by God in the Scriptures and made vibrant and relevant by the Spirit of God for every generation. This could surely be the most exciting and exhilarating time ever in the history of the church. We need to see a new vision of the rich eternal resources of God. We need to see a new vision of the church as God intended it to be. We need to see a new vision that will make us willing to change despite the pain.

And we need to hear a voice, a voice that says insistently and unequivocally, 'I will build my church.' Jesus came to establish a new society on earth. It was not enough for him to call individual sinners to repentance and to God. The church will be the most powerful force on earth provided it is inspired and sustained by his life and love and follows his pattern. Nothing could stop or ever has stopped the revolution of love and the reverberation of life which began two thousand years ago.

> Here is a man who was born in an obscure village, the child of a peasant woman. He never wrote a book. He never held an office. He never owned a home. He never went to college. He never travelled two hundred miles from the place he was born. He had no credentials but himself. He had nothing to do with the world except the naked power of his divine manhood. The tide of popular opinion turned against him. He was turned over to his enemies. He went through the mockery of a trial. He was nailed to a cross between two thieves. When he was dead, he was taken down from the cross and laid in a borrowed grave through the pity of a friend.
>
> Nineteen wide centuries have come and gone, but today he is the centrepiece of the human race and the leader of

the column of progress.

I am far with the mark when I say that all the armies that ever marched, and all the navies that were ever built, and all the parliaments that ever sat, and all the kings that ever reigned together, have not affected the life of man upon earth so powerfully as has that one solitary life.

God is doing a new thing in his church now. It is not new in the sense that God has never done it before, but in the sense that he loves to do the same thing differently. Just at a time when the forecast is bleak and hope seems long since to have disappeared beneath the horizon, God is proving again that what is impossible with men is possible with God. If our faith is in him and in the power of the risen, reigning Christ, we can certainly believe in the church which he will build, against which the organized hierarchy of the kingdom of darkness cannot prevail.

Let us sing a new song in the land of our fathers:

Rise up, O men of God!
Have done with lesser things;
Give heart and soul and mind and strength
To serve the King of kings.

2

'Hey—What Are You Up To?'

I had only been in my new home in the west of Scotland a few days when I discovered I had a problem. There was a heavy storm door in front of the glass front door which had a tendency to blow shut. It could only be opened by an enormous key which it would have been quite ridiculous to carry around. When I returned home as darkness fell one winter afternoon I discovered the storm door had blown shut. I was securely locked out! The house stood in a secluded private cul-de-sac at the end of a terrace of six houses.

I felt reasonably confident that by climbing onto the garden shed which was built on to the kitchen and crossing the kitchen roof I could quite easily reach the bathroom window. I had done this, and decided that the only thing I could do was to break a small pane of glass in the window and release the catch. As I carefully broke the glass I was aware of an agitated voice crying: 'Hey—what are you up to?' I was to discover later that this was one of our delightful neighbours—an elderly man who knew everything about everybody and everything. He was simply being a responsible citizen concerned about the property of his neighbours. Unfortunately he had jumped to a wrong conclusion. He thought I was a burglar breaking into this house!

The church has suffered severely in this century through having made wrong assumptions, jumping to wrong conclusions and then acting wrongly. I want to look at some of these wrong assumptions, so that our wrong conclusions can be corrected.

1. The church is a building

It seems almost banal to declare firmly that the church is not a building, but that it is people. However, the church's golden age of effectiveness was during the first three centuries of her life, when buildings were not a part of her existence. Malcolm Muggeridge, with characteristic incisiveness, writes:

> In an average English village today Anglican worship has become little more than a dying bourgeois cult. A small cluster of motorcars may be seen outside the parish church when a service is in progress; the bells still ring joyously across the fields and meadows on Sunday mornings and evenings, but fewer and fewer heed them and those few predominantly middle-class, female and elderly . . . It must be desperately disheartening, and the incumbent often gives the impression of being dispirited and forlorn. Whatever zeal he may have had as an ordinand soon gets dissipated in an atmosphere of domestic care and indifference on the part of his flock. Small wonder, then, that in the pulpit he has little to say except to repeat the old traditional clerical banalities as invariable as jokes in *Punch*; sometimes, in deference to the twentieth century, lacing the sad brew with references to the United Nations, apartheid and the birth pill. He doubtless feels himself to be redundant. The villagers stoically die without his ministrations; they would resent any interruption of their evening telly if he ventured to make a call, and have for long accustomed themselves to cope without the benefit of

> clergy with minor misfortunes like pregnancy and delinquency. In the large cities the situation is not dissimilar.[3]

You may consider that observation to be acid and cynical—or perceptive, shrewd and honest—depending on your point of view. The fact remains, however, that for many both outside as well as inside the church that building of Norman, Victorian or twentieth century architecture is the church. That is its visible evidence! What goes on within it gives it significance or otherwise.

The word 'church' occurs only twice in the gospels. It is used by Jesus in the controversial passage where he says he would build his church 'on this rock' (Mt 16:18), as well as in the passage where Jesus is speaking about church discipline and instructs them that the sin of an unrepentant member should be shared with the church (Mt 18:17).

Our English word 'church'—like the German *kirche,* Swedish *kyrka,* Slav *cerkov* and Scottish *kirk*—comes from the Byzantine Greek *kurike,* which means 'belonging to the Lord'. Several European languages, however, derive their word for 'church' from the Greek *ekklesia.* The French *eglise,* Spanish *iglesia,* Italian *chiesa,* Latin *ecclesia* and Welsh *egewys* all come from this root.

For the Greeks the meaning was clear: the word was a reference to 'those people who had been called out'. *Ekklesia* came from two Greek words: *ek* meaning 'out of' and *cletoi,* meaning 'called' or 'summoned'. The Hebrew word *qhal,* which is translated over seventy times by *ekklesia* in the Greek translation of the Old Testament, comes from a root which means 'to summon'. Israel were God's summoned or called out ones. God said of them: 'When Israel was a child, I loved him and called him out of Egypt as my son.'

What a marvellous anticipation of the New Covenant church that is! They were released from physical slavery in Egypt (which represents, in the Bible, the kingdom of this world). It was a physical shadow of the spiritual exodus from sin that the Christian church experiences. It was wholly a sovereign act of God. Israel was utterly unable to get released by herself from her slavery. It was the marvellous and miraculous intervention of God that freed them. The Old Testament record of Israel's captivity, their release, and their subsequent pilgrimage to the land that God had provided for them is the greatest record of escape in all of human history. It is preserved for us in the book of Exodus—the great escape! God called out Israel, impoverished and helpless, to enable his people to become what he wanted them to be so that they could demonstrate clearly to the rest of creation what he is like.

So the church belongs to God, has come from God, and owes every good gift that it enjoys to God. Without the love of God, the initiative of God, the salvation, revelation and call of God, there would be no church.

That well-known and highly articulate Roman Catholic, Hilaire Belloc, marvelled that when he considered the manner in which the Roman Church had been led, he realized that it was thanks to God that it had survived at all. Undoubtedly the same can be said for the other historic and denominational expressions of the church's life. Yet for all its crass stupidity, crimes and weaknesses (which are only to be expected from what clearly is and always has been a fellowship of sinners), the church has constantly received the sheer undeserved generosity of the heart of God shining irresistibly through the darkness and gloom of human imperfections.

All this has nothing to do with buildings, but everything to do with people—people who have been called out and clearly summoned by God, and who now belong to God, demonstrating his sovereignty and grace and displaying his power and love. The church comprises people who have been wonderfully released from the harassment, domination and restraint of the world's values, pressures and anxieties and who have been brought gloriously to a place where they are now able to be instructed by his wisdom, inspired by the revelation of his love and grace, corrected by his truth and righteousness, and respond to it all in practical living. The church will never know power or success as long as it aims at a building filled with people. It will only know reality and relevance when it aims at people filled with the Holy Spirit.

How I grieve over the amount of money, time, energy, discussion, argument and emotion spent on buildings. Of course buildings have their function in the contemporary church, but they are not of the essence of the church.

Two profoundly meaningful things have happened within our own church within very recent times. One was the removal of the pews from the whole of the downstairs area (to be replaced by chairs) without any discussion or debate. Those responsible for the fabric of the church handled this carefully and responsibly. I regarded this as a major breakthrough in our life together and evidence of some measure of maturity, since we were no longer upset by building changes, since buildings are not of the essence of the church.

The other thing was the freedom to put up outside our building a notice saying, *Gold Hill Baptist Church meets here.* When there are no people in the building it is not a church, it is simply a building. In spite of all that unconsciously slips into our conversation, both in praying and preaching, the church building is not the house of God. In the Old Testament God certainly dwelt in buildings, but in the New Testament God clearly is declared to dwell in people.

While God waits for his temple to be built of the lives of human beings and the love of human hearts, men bring stones and concentrate on architects and builders, shape and size. Duncan Campbell, whom God used so singularly in the revival that came to the Western Isles of Scotland in the middle of this century, said: 'What the world needs to see is the wonder of God-possessed personalities; men and women with the life of God pulsating within, who practise the presence of God and consequently make it easy for others to believe in God.'[4]

2. A large church is bad news

Most of us have been part of small struggling fellowships, coping with internal strife and external ineffectiveness for such a long time that we regard this as normal. When confronted with a spiritual success story we try to discover some flaw; some transitory human explanation; some factor which is suspect and open to condemning criticism—because surely such things are abnormal and not to be welcomed. Difficulties with internal relationships and tension there will always be, and a limited impact on a godless and word-soaked society is a fact of life, but we must not rationalize our failure in such a way that failure becomes success and success becomes suspect.

From time to time I hear two biblical incidents being cited within our own church. It always occurs when God is giving us a bigger view of his purposes. The first is the record of Gideon, one of God's heroes in the book of Judges. He began with a volunteer group of 32,000 and reduced it to a band of 300 in order to be effective against their enemies, the Midianites. The other incident is that of Jesus dying alone upon the cross, because he declared to the great crowds drawn by his preaching that to follow him required dedication and involved pain and sacrifice.

Surely Gideon was a hero, and God used him to defeat the Midianites and secure his purpose. His strategy was all part of God's plan for his people of that day in that situation. However, to make that wartime strategy a model for all time in either warfare or evangelism is silly. In any case, for each example of how Gideon handled the situation the Bible has many, many more examples of Joshua's battle tactics. He threw as many warriors as possible into the thick of the battle. This was costly, but effective! Throughout history wars have generally been won by large armies, and evangelism has generally been effective when the Lord has thrust out labourers into the harvest field in significant numbers.

Jesus, too, was concerned with growth and development. When he talked about the kingdom of God, he spoke of a tiny mustard seed—so small that it is difficult to see it—which would eventually develop into a great tree some eight to twelve feet high (Mt 13:31-32). While the church is not the kingdom of God, it is part of God's strategy for building his kingdom.

Jesus began by winning twelve people to himself. At the end of his earthly ministry that twelve had become 120, but more probably upwards of 500—as is hinted in 1 Corinthians 15:6. But that growth rate was sustained. The early believers did not say, 'Now let's reduce that 120 back to twelve so that we can be effective in evangelism.' Instead they waited and had a remarkable ten-day prayer meeting until all 120 were filled with the Holy Spirit. This tiny, hesitant, vulnerable organism then became remarkably effective in growth. In one day they grew from 120 to 3,120. The fact that there was considerable quantity did not seem to reduce their quality. They 'spent their time in learning from the apostles, taking part in the fellowship, and sharing in the fellowship meals and the prayers. Many miracles and wonders were done through the apostles, and everyone was filled with awe . . . and every day the Lord added to their group those who were being saved'. This was clearly no nine days' wonder, but a new fact of daily life. Luke does not quantify numbers or time-span, but two chapters later on he does tell us that though the first persecution struck them and Peter and John found themselves in prison, it was not before they had won another 5,000 men. Presumably women were in addition to this.

The course of early church history continues with whole communities being won to Christ; the Gentiles being touched by the gospel as well as the Jews; and new continents being opened to the good news of Jesus. As we move towards the end of Acts Paul reports to the mother church in Jerusalem, and there is a response from the leaders there that 'you can see how many thousands of Jews have become believers'. The word 'thousands' in this passage comes from a Greek word *muriades* (myriads), which actually means tens of thousands. In other words, the Apostle Paul, whose main evangelistic thrust was towards the Gentiles, was made aware that the number of Jews who had become followers of Jesus could only be estimated in myriads or multiples of thousands. So the Jerusalem church which started with 3,120 on the day of Pentecost sustained its growth and development in an extraordinary way.

Jesus, whose stated goal was making disciples, was a tremendous success for at least the next thirty years after he planted the first church and went to heaven. Not only did Jesus die on the cross for church growth and command church growth, but he also set an example for church growth through his ministry. To cite Jesus as an example of 'small is beautiful' is absurd.

It is easy to rationalize our failure to grow and develop by assuming that the ideal size of a church is between 200 and 250; by affirming that God is looking for godliness, not growth (when in fact he is looking for both!); by putting most of our effort into consolidating believers rather than winning unbelievers; by citing Gideon's band in the Old Testament and failure at the cross in the New Testament.

The facts of the matter are that Jesus taught his disciples to pray, 'May your kingdom come; may your will be done on earth as it is in heaven,' and the heart of God was revealed when his servant spoke of the 'glory of the Lord covering the earth as the waters cover the sea'. Let us be careful that we do not glorify smallness and quality and consequently regard growth in numbers as disreputable. Let us stand firmly against the accusation of cheap triumphalism when we are obeying the command of Jesus: 'Go, then, to all peoples everywhere and make them my disciples. . . .'

3. One pastor is the ideal arrangement

Within our western culture this assumption is widely made. When one tries to move into plurality of leadership and the development of a pastoral team with complementary, not duplicate, ministries, one becomes acutely aware of it. We have tried to do this in our own church, and in many ways I have been made aware of the congregation's preference for the 'old arrangement' of the one-man band. This would not be true of all of the congregation all of the time, but certainly some of the congregation some of the time. Within our own church this reaction is very loving and gracious, but it is nevertheless a fact.

It is said that in the United States a church will look for four gifts in a pastor. He will be a preacher of some distinction; a visitor of some diligence; an administrator of some acumen; and a youth worker of some acceptability. If you find a man with one of these gifts, then your church will stay as it is. If you find a pastor with two of these gifts your church will grow. If he has three of these gifts your church will quickly become the main one in town. If perchance he possesses all four, don't touch him, because he is liable to be a freak.

It is never God's pattern to assume or indeed to insist that one pastor is the best arrangement, and so steps need to be taken and restrictions laid down to ensure that it works tolerably well. I am frequently asked, 'How many ministers do you have, then, at your church?' I always reply, 'We have five pastors and more than 500 ministers!' This is not an attempt to be smart, but to enforce correct biblical thinking. The man has never been born (apart from Jesus) who has all the gifts for ministry and leadership. Indeed in our present church situation we are still painfully aware of a dearth of some gifts among us that would make us a more relevantly functioning body of Christ.

The apostles had clearly come to terms with their ministry and calling under God. When this was threatened they took immediate steps to ensure that it was preserved. 'It is not right,' they said, 'for us to neglect the preaching of God's word in order to handle finances' (Acts 6:2). Preaching God's word was not an easy option which allowed them an excuse from being involved in other activities. It was their calling under God and resulted in a dramatic penetration of the truth of God into a rigid, legalistic, proud and lifeless religious system and ultimately into a godless pagan society (cf. Acts 2:14; 3:12; 4:1; 4:8; 4:17,18).

The 'small is beautiful' attitude to the church, combined with the 'one-man band' system of ministry and leadership, leads quickly to that awesome phenomenon of 'playing at churches'. It causes our society to look at us and conclude:

> They do it every Sunday,
> They'll be all right on Monday,
> It's just a little habit they've acquired.

To insist on maintaining a fellowship at between 150 to 250 just about gives a church the ability to cope financially with buildings, equipment, minimal part-time help and interest in mission both at home and abroad, along with one pastor. But there is little on-going progress in the church's ministry.

From the pastor's point of view, he discovers that he can only cope with the system (though there are notable exceptions) by moving from one church to another about every three to ten years. During that time he has exhausted his usefulness to that congregation because the areas of gifts and ministries which he does not possess have now become obvious. It is a significant feature of church growth that a substantial number of pastors of growing churches have considered their particular parish or congregation to be a lifetime calling. They are not looking for greener pastures, but are concerned to raise up alongside them gifts and ministries in which they are deficient, but are necessary for the on-going growth and development of that particular part of the body of Christ. 'Such pastors,' says C. Peter Wagner, 'are excited about what they are doing, and they are fulfilled in their ministry. They love the people as much as the people love them. They do not regularly ask themselves. "Could it be that my ministry here is ending?" Pastors of growing churches are generally characterised by longevity in the ministry.'

It is a sad and culpable feature of the training in our

theological colleges in the United Kingdom that little is done to excite the concept of functioning 'body-life' and complementary team ministry. Many are trained to be professional leaders, having undergone academic disciplines. My own training for the ministry ensured that I knew how to pass exams and gain academic qualifications, but gave little experience of the work that God was ultimately to give me to do.

Recently I was ministering in Indonesia and I heard of a theological seminary there which insisted that each of its new students had planted one church of one hundred members, and that he had won thirty of them to Christ personally. It is little wonder that this fifth most populous country in the world with five large and 3,000 small inhabited islands with twenty-five major language groups has known the touch of God in a significant way in revival. One of these islands, Irian Jaya, has a population of one million. It is a wild undeveloped part of the country with small tribes emerging from a stone-age culture among its peoples—yet God has moved in a remarkable way, and 70% of the population is Christian. I realize that the Indonesian culture is quite different from ours, but this must cause us to pause for thought.

4. The local church has a limited geographical responsibility

There is scant biblical foundation for insisting on rigid territorial boundaries for any local church. It may help administration and practical operating, but to criticize a church which is operating outside what is considered its legitimate and normal boundaries is to be in danger of frustrating the purposes of God to bring life where death is reigning, reality where formalism has got the upper hand, and hope where despair has invaded human hearts. It is popular to look askance at growth by addition rather than multiplication. When a number of people leave church A to join church B, church B is accused of 'sheep-stealing'. In many cases, it might be much better described as 'sheep-finding'. The 'stolen' sheep might have continued on their formal, lack-lustre mediocrity towards spiritual atrophy had they not been 'found' and lovingly included into a warm, realistic congregation of God's people.

I was challenged at depth in my own thinking when I noticed that in the vibrant, developing Acts story 'the group of believers was one in mind and heart' (Acts 4:32). Their fellowship was based on a spiritual awareness of one another rather than by the fact that they lived within an area circumscribed by a felt-tipped pen drawn on an estate-agent's map.

It is of pressing importance to look closely at the reasons for this assumption that any local church ought to fix its boundaries on a geographical basis of approximately a two-mile radius around the church building where for the most part it functions. I want to list some of the causes of this wrong assumption to stimulate your thinking.

1. It is caused by insecurity among those involved in a particular local church. God has not called us to dig ourselves in and defend our territory against our allies, but to plan ways and means whereby we may actively and consistently plunder enemy territory. I have found little concern over this issue within local churches where numbers are comparatively high and where there is a dominating desire to win people to Jesus Christ as Lord and Saviour.

2. The assumption is based on a concept of church-planting which is human rather than divine and has often led to spiritual poverty (and often material struggles too!) and a waste of money and energy both

abroad and at home. It begins with a leadership structure rather than spiritual life in people.

3. It frequently has a high profile of denominational competition and pride. The great question in these godless, disturbing days is not whether my denomination has a presence in that community or not, but rather whether there is a realistic and significant evidence of the body of Christ on earth there.

4. Geographical limitation of the scope of the local church is inevitably outmoded, because of the new mobility in any community. If I work in one community, this is liable to be different from the community where I sleep. After all, we do speak quite freely of dormitory communities. Mobility is one of the features of our society. However we may regret the break-up of closely-knit community life and the advent of the motor car, both are social phenomena which cannot be disregarded.

5. There is a lack of understanding of what Luke calls *homothumadon* ('one mind', Acts 2:46) as a feature of the new, developing organism of the church. This 'one-mindedness' is not an agreement or assent to an external denominational constitution, but rather the acceptance and experiencing of an internal devotional commitment to Christ.

6. The beginnings of some churches hardly bear honest scrutiny. But they are now in existence and the years have passed and they demand local support. I can remember being involved with a church which had broken fellowship with another local church of a similar denominational colour over the issue of whether only the members of that church could share communion or whether the Lord's Table should be open to all Christians who confessed Jesus Christ as Lord and Saviour. Within two years the 'breakaway' local church had resolved the issue and accepted the practice of an 'open'

Communion Table, which was the conviction of the church with which it had broken fellowship. By then, however, it had established itself as a new local church amidst deep animosity and bitterness which was to continue in generations still to come. The requirement of that church was surely repentance rather than demanding recognition as a visible, functioning, local church.

7. Fixing rigid geographical boundaries involves a legalism which brooks no freedom of choice on the basis of personal or family need.

The results of this wrong assumption that the local church has a limited geographical scope are not difficult to discover. However, it is worth noting what they are in order to stimulate us to steer in a different direction, since they are so devastating and destructive.

1. The assumption has seriously restricted the visual image of the church within our society. There has been a significant decline in attendances at football matches throughout the country, and yet there is unavoidable evidence that a League Football match is being played in the town where that event is taking place. I lived for some years in two towns with football teams. In neither town was their team by any means a glamorous one, and yet it was almost impossible to park my car outside my house when a home match was taking place. Admittedly, in both cases we lived within a quarter of a mile of the football ground! However, in spite of a dramatic decline in church attendance, there are seven times more people attending church today in the United Kingdom than those who attend football matches.

2. It has persistently perpetuated historical divisiveness, thus cramping effective evangelism and nurturing a competitive spirit, when co-operation and fellowship are in fact required.

3. It has brought confusion to new converts to Chris-

tianity. Many within our post-Christian society are second-generation agnostics. The finer points of Christian doctrine elude them and some aspects of denominational tradition and practice have no meaning or relevance to their newly-found reality. Their desire is just that—the pursuit of real Christianity rather than the practice of religion.

4. It has fed spiritual pride and been the means of erecting often impenetrable denominational barriers. The fundamental importance of the centrality of Christ, the authority of Scripture, the practical outworking of biblical teaching, the significant movement of the Holy Spirit in renewal, the importance of fellowship and the plurality of leadership are all truths which are often put in second place to loyalty to traditional practices.

5. It has elevated divisive issues to a place which they do not deserve. Admittedly, there are issues where opinion will be divided, but that is not to justify the demanding place that these issues often assume. All my working life the top of the agenda in the church nationally and internationally has been ecumenism—often worthless in its theological content and doomed to disintegration because it was contrived and controlled by man. Now, however, the great concern is not ecumenism, but evangelism. There is a slow but sure awakening to the fact that we no longer live in a Christian country, but we as a nation are driving to hell in our Volvos and Mini Metros. No longer are we so concerned about committees as we are about conversions. No longer are we so obsessed by people inside the church as we are about the 98.5% of our fellow countrymen who are in reality outside the church. No longer are we so concerned with maintaining structures as we are in allowing the Spirit to have free course of action and to be glorified.

6. It has been responsible for a wicked and wasteful

use of manpower. As we said before, there are more clergy today per head of the population than there are doctors within our society.

5. Effective communication of truth can come through Sunday preaching and teaching

Within our own church we lay a heavy emphasis on teaching the word of God. Each Sunday morning at each of the services (apart from our monthly family service) we devote up to fifty minutes to consecutive exposition of a book of the Bible, a significant section of a book of the Bible or a biblical theme or doctrine. We attempt to make sure that the diet of teaching is balanced between Old Testament and New Testament; devotional and doctrinal; inspirational and practical; historical and theological. Our programme has frequent seminars on basic Christianity; life in the Spirit; leadership and commitment. These run concurrently with our second morning service. A great deal of time is spent considering the needs and tempo of the church's life and producing a relevant teaching programme.

I notice that Paul, the apostle and evangelist extraordinaire, adopted a vigorous teaching programme in Ephesus (Acts 19). He began in the synagogue with three months of discussion and teaching on the kingdom of God. Things became too hot to handle there, and so Paul moved to the lecture hall of Tyrannus. He remained there teaching and discussing the Christian faith every day for two years. That is a pretty heavy teaching programme by any standard, especially since some manuscripts add that this daily teaching diet lasted for five hours at a time. That is a significantly higher concentration of teaching than goes into a university or theological degree programme.

Truth, however, needs to be demonstrated as well as

declared if it is going to be grasped and embraced properly. Two senses, rather than one, need to be involved in an effective communication of truth—seeing as well as hearing. Truth needs not only to be understood, but obeyed and then shared if it is ever to become relevant and significant. It cannot be considered to have been truly communicated until that has been done.

Jesus in his Great Commission to the church did not simply command us to 'make disciples' and then 'baptize' them, but also to 'teach them to *obey* everything I have commanded you'. There are many excellent teaching programmes within the churches of the United Kingdom, but regrettably they seldom demand a response which can be monitored and observed. How important it is to recognize that effective teaching of the truth cannot come through Sunday teaching and preaching alone, and so there is a need to set up a structure within the church which emphasizes that truth taught is only valid when it issues in truth lived.

We have found the warmth, security, reality and freedom discovered in our house fellowships—which meet on Tuesdays so that church members can encourage one another to practise what has been preached—an enormous help in this area. This is not in any way to lose confidence in preaching, but it is to highlight the reality that truth taught needs to be lived—otherwise it has not been taught properly. Every teaching must have a 'therefore'.

6. Parking accommodation is of secondary importance

Many of us have inherited buildings which are not quite suitable for the kind of ministry and service God is giving us to share today. They are often restricting in their facilities and limited in their design. In addition they often pre-date the advent of the motorcar. Public transport has now declined significantly in scope and reliability. Financial pressures on churches make the provision of adequate car-parking a less important requirement than the multitude of other facility and equipment needs. After all, in the past no parking had been necessary, and when it became so street parking sufficed.

I notice increasingly an insertion in the advertising of commercial enterprises that parking is not only available, but it is free. That is clearly a significant facility which is not to be missed. It is insulting and insensitive of us in the church to assume that car parking is 'their problem' and not ours, or alternatively to assume that 'they can walk'.

Within our own church the most consistent single difficulty we have faced over a number of years is car parking. Seldom do we have a Sunday without our services being interrupted because of illegal parking, 'creative' parking, or some other difficulty or infringement—all of this in spite of well-manned and diligent stewarding and the provision of alternative arrangements (admittedly not in close proximity to the church building). The irritation and hostility caused to our neighbours would be hard to measure, but surely it has affected our witness in our immediate environs.

This, as much as any other, has been a major motivation for us to look for new premises in which to administer and control our life together. After searching the area meticulously we have managed to purchase nineteen-and-a-half acres of land which (planning authorities' permission permitting) we would hope to develop not only for building but for adequate car parking. The disruption and cost will reach enormous proportions, but the need demands it. For us, other solutions have not worked properly. 'Bussing' people from home and transporting them by minibus from distant car parks have created as many problems as they have solved.

To assume that car parking is a matter of secondary importance is to grossly underestimate the effect that it has.

7. The gifts of the Holy Spirit are not for today

It is one thing to say, 'I do not manifest any of the gifts of the Holy Spirit—in so far as I understand what they are!' It is quite another thing to say, 'Therefore the gifts of the Holy Spirit are not valid or viable today.' It has been assumed that their absence in experience has indicated their absence in reality. It is a dangerous and destructive thing to build a theology on experience—or the lack of it. Such has been my own background, both through liberal theology (which rationalizes the supernatural) and dispensational theology (which limits many aspects of the supernatural to the pages of the Old and New Testaments).

There are actually three views (in the evangelical sphere) regarding the gifts of the Holy Spirit:

1. The gifts were given to the church to 'get it going'. Having succeeded in such a remarkable way, they were then withdrawn, since we no longer required them to endorse the message proclaimed or to exhibit the reality preached.

2. The gifts were not permanently withdrawn, but emerge only at the discretion of the Spirit himself. The consequence is that they will appear and disappear from age to age and from generation to generation.

3. The gifts are valid today. They are to be sought, received and used for the glory of God in the enriching of the body of his Son on earth—the church.

Clearly from the New Testament we are called as Christians to manifest the *character* of Christ—and this we do as the Holy Spirit produces his fruit in us. But we are also called to manifest the *conduct* of Christ—and this we do as the Holy Spirit releases his gifts to us. All in all the Spirit's ministry is to exalt Jesus—and this he does in us and through us by his fruit and gifts.

A gift of the Holy Spirit is not significant on its own, but only so far as it relates to the body of Christ and reveals the person of Christ. Truth proclaimed needs also to be truth portrayed. Character and conduct are the means whereby this is possible and real.

I like the word 'gift' since it emphasizes that God's blessings can never be earned, nor are they ever deserved. However, 'gift' hardly does justice to the rich word which it translates. The word *charisma* comes from perhaps the loveliest word in Christian vocabulary—*charis,* or 'grace'. The gifts of the Holy Spirit are the expressions of God's grace, or the evidence of the sheer undeserved generosity of the heart of God. How very much we need and desire that today. How impoverishing it is when we make a wrong assumption about the gifts. We constantly need to examine the assumptions that we make lest we steer a wrong course in our lives and fail to see the will of God for his people.

3

'Please Come Together!'

The early church relied upon a three-fold witness as a means of reaching and impressing a cynical, unbelieving and word-proof world: proclamation (*kerygma*) which was direct, uncomplicated and authoritative by modern standards; demonstration (*dunameis* and *semeia* — powers and signs) which was irrefutable, life-transforming and impressive by any standard and fellowship (*koinonia*) which was spontaneous, warm, and utterly supernatural. They had learned the meaning and the reality of the third part of 'the Grace'—'the fellowship of the Holy Spirit'. The combination of these three made their witness powerful and effective.

Pagans could shrug off the proclamation as simply another 'teaching' among many. To their own satisfaction they could explain away the demonstration as simply a natural phenomenon for which they had not yet full understanding. However it was, and is, much more difficult to reject the evidence of fellowship. The practical, active concern of Christians for each other and their evident awareness of sharing life—with all the tensions that brought in rethinking and restyling life—in the same great family of God as valued brothers and sisters left the pagan world drooling with envy. It prompted the often-quoted remark of a pagan writer—'How these Christians love one another.'

Two very clear principles emerge quickly in the book of Acts and remain right through to the end. First of all, that God chooses people for his purposes. He did not need to, but he obviously did so. He might well have used angels or natural phenomena. Had he done so, he would then at least have been in direct control! But God chose to use ordinary, unspectacular, unlikely men and women. I remember my old teacher, William Barclay of Trinity College, Glasgow, repeatedly saying in his gruff, rasping, direct way: 'God doesn't use extraordinary people to do extraordinary things—God uses ordinary people to do ordinary things in an extraordinary way.'

Only two apostles appear with any real impact in Acts. The other ten no doubt were involved, but are not named, apart from John (who never speaks!) and James (who is quickly beheaded!). The first half of the book is really about Peter. He and John are described as 'ordinary men of no education' (*agrammatoi . . . idiotai* — ungrammatical idiots!). The second half is mainly about Paul. Although quite different from Peter in background and ability—he was a university scholar involved in the housing programme—he was nevertheless a most unlikely character for God to use in view of his track record against the church.

The second clear principle which emerges right through Acts is that God uses individuals, but not individualists. An individual is a person with personality and gifts; different from others in a multitude of ways; distinguishable by appearance, temperament, background, ability and voice. An individualist is someone who either will not or cannot relate to others. He wants freedom to do what he wants, go where he wants and act as he feels. He is his own ultimate authority, whatever the situation. In Acts, however, there is a strong sense of relationship, fellowship, community and team. In fact in the Bible there is no such thing as solitary religion, and there is no evidence of unattached Christians anywhere in the New Testament. For many of us there needs to be a relearning of the nature and the need of fellowship. The sturdy independence instilled into many of us as an attractive and necessary social virtue in our Western society and underlined and emphasized spiritually by nineteenth century evangelicalism needs now to be challenged. No man is an island!

The contemporary church in the West, however, gives little evidence of this heart-warming, intimately-relating, society-challenging, life-transforming fellowship. It tends to be a rather snooty religious club defending its rules and demanding its fees. It has its own culture and sits rather uneasily when it is disturbed or challenged. It appears from time to time as a political action group monitoring how the political winds are blowing—often much too late and confusedly emphasizing the wrong issue. It is largely dismissed by our contemporaries as a non-segregated waiting room for the next bus to heaven. For many it appears as a kind of low-calorie dessert for those who want a bit extra which will not hurt their lifestyle or affect their public image. For others it is a gathering of spiritual junkies having their weekend religious 'fix'. For some it is an offensive religious democracy unacceptably trying to legislate for the morals of the rest of the world.

So far as God is concerned, however, fellowship is never an end in itself—it is for a purpose. The purpose God intended is that we should be the new body of Christ on earth. In the gospel of Luke we have the Acts of Jesus Volume I—in the Acts of the Apostles we have the Acts of Jesus Volume II. In the gospel of Luke we have all that Jesus *began* to do—in the Acts of the Apostles we have what Jesus *continued* to do. All that had happened between Luke and Acts is that Jesus changed bodies. In Luke he lives his life in his incarnate body, conceived by the Holy Spirit and born of the Virgin Mary. In Acts he lives his life in his new body—the church—by the power of the Holy Spirit released in the lives of believers. It was into this new body that the same Holy Spirit came that he received at his baptism in the Jordan river. The Holy Spirit is spoken of forty times in the first twelve chapters of Acts. Clearly his teaching indicated that when people on earth are filled with this same Spirit of Jesus they can do the same things.

The linguistic expert Frank Laubach writes:

> When Christ was here on earth, He was limited to performing His ministry in one place and at one time. He was one man walking beside one sea in one little corner of the earth. He healed whoever He touched, but His touch was necessarily limited by time and space. Now, does it make sense that the Father would send His Son for this limited ministry? I don't think that is tenable. He made provision to carry on the work through the Holy Spirit: we are to complete His mission. We are His multiplied hands, His feet, His voice and compassionate heart. Imperfect and partial to be sure, but His healing Body just the same. It is through the Holy Spirit (Christ's love which is everywhere at once), that we receive the power to carry on the work of the apostles. It is a challenging and sobering thought: when we receive the Holy Spirit into our lives, we receive the same urgent and life-giving force that led our Master.[5]

The apostle Paul emphasizes no fewer than seven times in one chapter to the Corinthian Christians (1 Corinthians 14) the absolute importance of a gift being used to glorify Christ and build up and enrich his new body on earth. Otherwise the gifts of the Holy Spirit become occasions of self-display and personal exhibitionism. Arnold Bittlinger wrote:

> Gifts are functions of the Body of Christ. They are His eyes, hands and feet, with which He acts and moves on earth. When gifts are no longer an expression of Christ's actions, then they are not only useless, but harmful in their effect. They are counterfeits which offer my neighbour nothing, but positively deceive him.[6]

How important it is, then, to see that fellowship is the way by which the true life of the body of Christ will be expressed to a broken, divided world, and the gifts of the Holy Spirit are given to ensure the relevance of that body in the midst of society. Clear, biblical teaching on this subject is essential lest this whole area lead to deception and counterfeits, abuses and tragedies. It is no wonder that some Christian leaders prefer to keep clear of this altogether. Yet fellowship remains fundamental to the revelation of the heart of God, and the gifts of the Holy Spirit secure relevance for that fellowship before a needy world. This is why the early church had such a powerful and penetrating witness. 'With great power,' says Luke, 'the apostles gave witness to the resurrection of the Lord Jesus, and God poured rich blessings on them all.' But that bold, dramatic, thrilling statement is within the direct context that

> The group of believers was one in mind and heart. No one said that any of his belongings was his own, but they all shared with one another everything they had . . . There was no one in the group who was in need. Those who owned fields and houses would sell them, bring the money received from the sale, and hand it over to the apostles; and the money was distributed to each one according to his need (Acts 4:32-35).

This is one of the most powerful and practical expressions and examples of fellowship in the whole Bible. It is so direct and down to earth that some have criticized it and dismissed it as nothing less than a practical expression of Communist political dogma—no private property, nobody owned anything, and distribution to each according to his need.

Nothing could be less related to the truth, however. Christianity and Communism are poles apart. Although Karl Marx, like Jesus, was a Jew drawing deeply from the teaching and bold insights of the Old Testament prophets, the conclusions he arrived at had nothing to do with the Spirit of God, but resulted in a rigid, man-made political system. Christianity is motivated and inspired by the love of God touching and transforming the heart of man, whereas Communism is a political system incapsulated and maintained in the rigid dictates of a legalism from the head. The passage itself (Acts 4:31-35) displays the very clear differences:

1. The fellowship of believers was 'one in mind and heart'. They were motivated by love, not by law. There was no force exerted and no religious KGB or secret police to scrutinize and enforce.

2. They were 'all filled with the Holy Spirit' (v. 31). The implication of that phrase is that they enjoyed, experienced and expected a daily filling of the life and power of God. It was not just their minds, emotions and wills that were affected—there is also an essential spiritual dimension. Communism as a philosophy and a political system is by definition atheistic and eliminates God and his Spirit totally from its thinking and practice.

3. 'They all shared with one another everything they had.' In other words there was a great spontaneity about their behaviour. This was the climate of their fellowship. They were not told or compelled to do this. This was not a good idea which had to be organized and

then implemented. There was no attitude of, 'Do we have to?', but rather an atmosphere which caused them to ask the question, 'How can we demonstrate the reality of our relationship with and our commitment to our brothers and sisters in the family of God?'

4. Property was neither in the hands of the state nor the church. 'Before you sold the property, it belonged to you; and after you sold it the money was yours' (Acts 5:4). They did not abolish private property because of a principle which had been taught and learned. They did so in order to be effective in their relationship and commitment to one another in practice.

5. These early Christians achieved what Communism never has. The operating principle of early Christian fellowship clearly was, 'From each according to his ability to each according to his need.' That may well be the stated Communist aim, but we have seen that the practice is: 'From each according to his ability to each according to his work.' The ideal can only be translated into reality by the ministry of the Holy Spirit, not by political dreaming.

6. Quite clearly the functioning of Christian fellowship here is based on a compassionate concern for the poor and disadvantaged. To confess Jesus as Lord and to live accordingly in a pagan society was to be unable to continue in the many kinds of employment available, and so the familiar way of earning a living had to be left. Such a clear profession in other cases was offensive to the state religion of emperor worship. For either or both these reasons many within the early church became unemployed and needed to be cared for in the absence of any social services programme. Hence the great opportunities to demonstrate compassionate concern within Christian fellowship. Communism, by contrast, is based on a hatred of the rich rather than concern for the poor.

7. The living presence of Christ in the power of the Holy Spirit was exercised locally, whereas classical Communism operates universally.

Any attempt to duck the realistic, practical implications of Spirit-initiated and maintained fellowship by the scare-mongering cry that it is simply thinly-veiled Communism is unacceptable. The deep implications of fellowship can only be faced in terms of the gracious, supernatural ministry of the Holy Spirit within us and among us. This needs to be picked up and implemented at some level in every local fellowship—or else the life we profess and the message we proclaim is bogus. No longer is 'billiard-ball' Christianity accepted (i.e. we touch one another for the shortest possible time and in the slightest possible way and then head in different directions). It is not possible to be equally committed to every Christian, so the practicalities must first be worked out in local areas and in small groups in order to be realistic.

Unity has been restored and made possible for us through the cross of Jesus Christ, not only between us and God, but also between us and us. In Genesis chapter 3 man's fellowship with God is destroyed as a result of man's sinful disobedience. In chapter 4, as surely as night follows day, man's fellowship with man is destroyed. On the cross Jesus not only reconciled man to God, but also brought man into a new and supernatural relationship with man.

While God has made it possible our task is to 'do your best to preserve the unity which the Spirit gives'. Fellowship needs to be given a context and climate in which to express itself. Dutiful service is not enough in today's cold and impersonal world. Often a touch, an arm around the shoulder, a warm handshake, a gentle embrace or a gracious smile which speaks from a loving heart can both express and increase the reality of love within the body of Christ. If it is God's love that is flowing, it is important to make sure that these expressions of love are genuine and in the Spirit. A great deal of the accusation of the church being 'God's frozen people' is due to the inbuilt reserve that is a cultural characteristic of the British—and of some other nations, too!

Within our own congregation house fellowships have begun to provide a context and climate for the expression of real fellowship. Historically, wherever the Spirit of God has been allowed to move in power and effectiveness there have been small group meetings. These have become not simply a group of people coming together to share ideas, but rather a group getting together to share their lives. The renaming of our house groups as house fellowships was not an exercise in semantics, but rather an exercise in describing and desiring real fellowship. The more the church grows, the more essential this becomes.

The Communist revolution of this century has demanded unhesitating obedience. An American student wrote a letter to his fiancée breaking off their engagement:

> We Communists have a high casualty rate. We are the ones who get shot at, hung, jailed, lynched, tarred and feathered, slandered, ridiculed, and fired from our jobs, and in every other way made as uncomfortable as possible. A certain percentage of us get killed or imprisoned; we live in virtual poverty. We turn back to the Party every penny we make above what is necessary to keep us alive.
>
> We Communists don't have the time or money for many movies or concerts or T-bone steaks or decent homes or new cars. We've been described as fanatics; we are fanatics. Our lives are dominated by one overshadowing factor: the struggle for World Communism!

> We Communists have a philosophy of life which no amount of money could buy. We have a cause to fight for, a definite purpose in life. We subordinate our petty personal selves into a great movement for humanity. There is one thing about which I am in earnest: the Communist cause! It is my life, my business, my religion, my hobby, my sweetheart, my wife, my mistress, my bread and my meat! I work at it in the daytime and dream of it at night! Therefore I cannot carry on a friendship, a love affair, or even a conversation, without relating everything to this force which both guides and drives my life . . . I have already been in jail because of my ideas, and if necessary I am ready to go before a firing squad.[7]

No wonder the Bolshevik Revolution based on Marx and Lenin's teaching, insights and philosophy has swallowed up more than half the world since 1917. The same intensity of devotion is demonstrated in the Islamic fundamentalism that is a powerful part of the contemporary scene. These movements have an inherent demand for full-blooded discipleship and a totally new way of living. Within it is an expression of commitment to one another, as well as commitment to the cause, which is practical and awesomely powerful.

In that same Acts passage (Acts 4:32-37) there is not only a record of the church's life in public, but also a delightful and moving expression of the church's life in private. Wherever Barnabas appears in the New Testament there is a bigness about him. He had a big mind—he courageously always thought the best about people. He had a big heart and his nature vindicated the name that his parents gave him. He constantly and creatively encouraged people; he was a true 'son of encouragement'. He also had an open hand—he never held tightly what rightfully belonged to him.

There are only two people—apart from Jesus—who in the New Testament are called *good* men. Both of them are called Joseph. One was Joseph of Arimathea and the other was Joseph called Barnabas—our man here! One had a garden and the other had a field. Both said about each of these things, 'Lord, you can have it!' Good in Scripture means *generous*. It is actual benevolence and is not restricted to the mind. It is an active attitude to people.

Barnabas inspires us to consider what our attitude towards others is. I have discovered that in most churches there are often five attitudes towards possessions in the context of fellowship. There are those who conclude that it is quite legitimate to say, 'What is mine is my own—I have earned it, saved it, legally been given it—it belongs to me. It's mine!' Understandable this may well be, but legitimate within Christian fellowship it can never be, however human and natural it is. Either implicitly or quite overtly this is a firm conviction of many Christians in the western world.

A second attitude is, 'What is yours is mine.' How often this form of blackmail is foisted on the church. It creates guilt and confusion among Christians when a needy one demands this kind of response. However, privilege is based on responsibility and Christian fellowship is motivated by love and not by a harsh, demanding legalism. Christian generosity is the spontaneous expression of the love of Christ from the heart and is never imposed from without.

A third attitude is, 'What is mine is yours.' In the first flush of my own personal discovery of new and deep relationships made by the Spirit of God creating fellowship at a level I had never known before, I was persuaded that this was a godly attitude. It may well be a vast improvement on the first two attitudes, but one of the elders in the church came alongside me with a gentle challenge when he heard me teach it. Graciously he corrected me, saying it was not so much that I was wrong as that I was not quite right.

There is another attitude which he implanted in my heart: 'What is mine is ours.' It is not so much that I give away what I have, but that I share it fully with my brothers and sisters.In doing so I may well 'give away' much of what I have, but the emphasis is not so much on my giving as it is on our sharing. This is a clear, practical expression of biblical fellowship under the lordship of Christ and direction of his Spirit.

However, we have not yet reached the distinctively Christian attitude towards possessions until we are able to say: 'What is mine is his (God's).' This alone will satisfy my attitude of discipleship and dependence upon the Lord. This alone will remove any suspicion of wrong motives in my relationship to my Christian brothers and sisters.

Some years ago a young vital preacher came to our home and blessed us with his warmth, friendship and godliness. It wasn't until later I discovered that though he had come to our country on the invitation of the evangelicals, he subsequently proved something of an embarrassment to them. I doubt if that would be so now, but his visit was a landmark in my own personal life, the life of my family, and the development of our church. He spoke to Christian leaders whom we gathered together one afternoon, and to a public meeting in the evening. I had never known the touch of God in that way before among us. His name was Juan Carlos Ortiz from Argentina. He said:

> The Bible said the kingdom of God is like a merchant looking for fine pearls. When he finds a pearl of real worth, he sells everything he has and buys that pearl. Of course, according to traditional thinking, man is the pearl of great price and Jesus the merchant who sells everything to make the purchase. Now I understand that *he* is the pearl of great price, and the man the merchant.

So when man finds Jesus, it costs him everything. Jesus has happiness, joy, peace, healing, security, eternity. Man marvels at such a pearl and says, 'I want this pearl. How much does it cost?'

The seller says, 'It's too dear, too costly.'

'But how much?'

'Well, it's very expensive.'

'Do you think I could buy it?'

'Oh, of course. Anybody can.'

'But you say it's too expensive. How much is it?'

'It costs everything you have—no more, no less—so anybody can buy it.'

'I'll buy it.'

'What do you have? Let's write it down.'

'I have 10,000 dollars in the bank.'

'Good, 10,000 dollars. What else?'

'I have nothing more. That's all I have.'

'Have you nothing more?'

'Well, I have some dollars here in my pocket.'

'How many?'

'I'll see: 30, 40, 50, 80, 100, 120—120 dollars.'

'That's fine. What else do you have?'

'I have nothing else. That's all.'

'Where do you live?'

'I live in my house.'

'The house too.'

'Then you mean I must live in the garage?'

'Have you a garage, too? That too. What else?'

'Do you mean I must live in my car, then?'

'Have you a car?'

'I have two.'

'Both become mine. Both cars. What else?'

'Well, you have the house, the garage, the cars, the money, everything.'

'What else?'

'I have nothing else.'

'Are you alone in the world?'

'No, I have a wife, two children . . .'

'Your wife and your children too.'

'Too?'

'Yes, everything you have. What else?'

'I have nothing else, I am left alone now.'

'Oh, you too. Everything. Everything becomes mine: wife, children, house, garage, cars, money, clothing, everything. And you too. Now you can use all those things here, but don't forget they are mine, as you are. When I need any of the things you are using you must give them to me because now I am the owner.'[8]

Powerful, penetrating stuff, and a salutary reminder that if we are concerned to live under the dynamic reign of God (i.e. to enter the kingdom of God) we must die to ourselves. Many Christians want to keep on doing their own thing after they are saved. It is for this reason that Jesus says that if we want to live we need to be prepared to die, for it is in losing our lives that we find them. This is why Jesus says that those who want to save their own lives are going to lose them. Many people who come to church want to live their own lives in many aspects without any direct reference to Jesus. It is not possible to do so and to be really relevant and effective. It doesn't work! Unhappily many of us settle for the fact that it doesn't work! What is mine is God's—the implications of this are profound and transforming for us, for God, and for others.

Releasing ownership of what we possess is not an end in itself. It is the means whereby we display and declare our commitment to Jesus Christ in real terms and express and experience the reality of Christian fellowship. Christian fellowship is wonderfully, practically and totally supernatural.

Having shown us what fellowship was like 'behind closed doors' in the early church (Acts 4:32-37), including its serious blemishes (Acts 5:1-11), Luke goes on to record its impact upon a broken, bewildered world.

This was Christianity—the real thing—being demonstrated for the very first time in history (Acts 5:12-16).

There were six remarkable evidences of God's life flowing among God's people:

1. There were 'many miracles and wonders being performed among the people by the apostles'. People were able not only to hear what the power of Christ could do, they were able also to see it unmistakably with their own eyes.

2. There was complete unity in the church. 'All the believers met together in Solomon's Porch.' Visible unity at a local level was not something they discussed, debated or prayed for—it was visible and real for all to see. With all the pressures externally and internally, this could only be attributed to the supernatural.

3. There was a very clear boundary and demarcation between believers and unbelievers—not in a foolish, arrogant or pretentious way, but as a result of inescapable reality. 'Nobody outside the group dared join them, even though the people spoke highly of them.' It was not that society wrote them off as a group of unrealistic, religious cranks, but rather the reality of God was so patently obvious and at work as to be unmistakable, and that created an attitude and atmosphere of holy awe.

4. Evangelism was as effective among men as it was among women: 'More and more people were added to the group—a crowd of men and women who believed on the Lord.' All through the years it has been my experience that often it is easier to win a woman to Christ than to win a man to Christ. The increasing number of Christian women in a fellowship with non-Christian, and sometimes anti-Christian, husbands can create a real problem. I believe that women have a greater spiritual perception and awareness than men. It may have something to do with femaleness and the

potential for motherhood—I do not know. However, the response of women to Christ more readily than men makes it a fact to be reckoned with. In Acts, however, no such issue existed.

5. Sick people were healed. 'As a result of what the apostles were doing, sick people were carried out into the streets and placed on beds and mats so that at least Peter's shadow might fall on some of them as he passed by.' Often today Christians within the church have faith for sickness rather than for healing. How often Job's boils, Paul's thorn and Timothy's stomach have been cited when healing is under discussion. Epaphroditus and Trophimus are thrown in for good measure. All the while one fifth of the gospels is a record of healings or discussion which arises from it. Of the 3,779 verses in the gospels, 727 relate specifically to the healing of physical or mental illness and the resurrection of the dead. Except for the discussion of the miracles of Jesus in general, the attention devoted to his healing ministry is far greater than that devoted to any one kind of experience. Forty-one distinct instances of physical or mental healing are recorded in the four gospels. The whole thrust of the revelation of God is that his concern is to make men whole. Jesus did say, 'As the Father sent me, so send I you.'

6. Hell was plundered by this heaven-sent ministry: 'Crowds of people came in from the towns around Jerusalem, bringing those who were sick or who had evil spirits in them: and they were all healed.' The release of captives is part of the gospel of the kingdom. Where the dynamic reign of God is being established either individually or corporately, then demonic forces must retreat. This is not a ministry for histrionics and for the bizarre, but it is part of the evidence of and the establishment of normal New Testament Christianity. Jesus did promise to build his church and part of the

experience of its presence is that the gates of hell will be unable to prevail against it.

Such is the inevitable effect of reality in our relationships within the church—it leads to relevance and effectiveness in our relationships outside the church. Fellowship, then, is not simply a matter of personal, selfish indulgence, but it has clear social implications in power and effectiveness. God is looking for his new body on earth to be whole and clean so that he can use it to declare his word and to demonstrate his power. Proclamation *(kerygma)* and demonstration *(dunameis* and *semeia)* are very closely related to fellowship *(koinonia)*. No wonder our Lord spent his last moments before going across the Kidron Brook and on to the agonizing experience in the Garden of Gethsemane in that impassioned prayer to his Father:

> I pray that they may all be one, Father! May they be in us, just as you are in me and I am in you. May they be one, so that the world will believe that you sent me. I gave them the same glory you gave me, so that they may be one, just as you and I are one, so that they may be completely one, in order that the world may know that you sent me and that you love them as you love me.

This is the *real* Lord's prayer! As we watch and listen our hearts cry out to God the Father too: 'Father, hear his prayer and let his cry come to you.'

4

Who Is in Charge Here?

I was having dinner one Saturday evening with some young married couples in our beautifully prepared candle-lit hall, when a man burst in upon us demanding, 'Who is in charge here?' From time to time that has been the irate question of one of our neighbours who has come to us very upset because someone had parked a car carelessly and with little regard to the convenience or privacy of others. Often the question has been asked with an understandable belligerence and certainly with the intention of getting some action. Although on this occasion the car did not belong to any of us, car parking has, as I have already mentioned, become an increasing problem to us over the years, with services frequently interrupted and animosity created in the neighbourhood which has infringed our witness, no matter how hard we have tried to find a practical solution.

However, the question has a right ring about it because someone constantly needs to be responsible for any group of people whether large or small. It need not contain a harsh, nasty note, but a note of honour and honesty. Undoubtedly one of the most significant features of the work of God when it is relevant and effective is that God raises up leadership, sometimes to initiate his work, but always to oversee and further it. Ever since Satan rebelled he has sought to smuggle the sins of independence, disobedience and rebellion into the church of the living God, and these attitudes are still a prevalent danger.

In Acts God raised up both a Peter and a Paul, at different times and to ensure satisfactory leadership in different areas of ministry. Neither appeared to be likely candidates for the job in view of Peter's volatile instability and Saul of Tarsus's aggressive antipathy towards the church. Yet both, through the circumstances of life and by the not-so-gentle hand of God upon them, were moulded into leadership material which reaped rich dividends for the kingdom of God. I doubt that any missionary society, Bible college or local church would have looked at them twice as suitable material for Christian leadership. God surely does not see us the way men do—for he does not give us the jobs we are fit for, but fits us for the jobs he gives us. Both obviously learned the lesson of leadership well since they acknowledged it in relation to their own ministry and emphasized it as necessary for the health and well-being of the churches that they planted in the name of Jesus.

A crucial question which haunts the contemporary world is: 'What is the ideal form of government?' Our world is more or less divided in half by two forms of government—democracy and dictatorship. Neither has a biblical foundation, although in a variety of ways most of us have allowed or insisted on one or the other being practised in the church. In democracy every person has a right to have a say in government. The people shall choose and change their government when and if they feel like doing so. Certainly we live in a day when political democracy is under attack within our society. The insidious effect of anarchy and lack of respect for people and property is growing.

Political dictatorship has fared no better. History bears an eloquent testimony to the inherent and destructive difficulties of dictatorship. Perhaps in the climate of confusion which exists both in the world and the church we are ready to hear what God has to say about government and leadership. Always his insistence has been on theocracy. This is government by God himself. It is the biblical ideal for both church and state, but how can a godless state acknowledge it when a rebellious church will not accept it and so cannot legitimately demonstrate it?

God wants to carry out his rule through godly leadership, which in practical terms means that some shall be responsible for the leadership of others and both shall be responsible to Jesus Christ. A pastor with great courage, and with even greater spiritual insight, said to his congregation on one occasion: 'I will for ever be your servant, but you can never be my master.' The practical and spiritual implications of this will repay clear thinking and prolonged meditation.

I suspect that here in the West there is a confused understanding of leadership. It carries with it in our culture prestige, position, privilege, distinction and honour. It is seen to be a means whereby I can be assured of approval by others—even of my popularity with them. For some it is the means whereby they can have and exercise control over others. In other words it is a means whereby I can make up for certain deficiencies in my own character. In Bible times, however, leadership carried with it dangers, hardship, contempt, social disadvantage, rejection and persecution. This is why Paul had to write to Timothy (1 Tim 3:1) with encouragement, 'This is a true saying: if a man is eager to be a church leader, he desires an excellent work.'

Anyone in leadership today, or about to enter leadership, needs to ask a fundamental question: 'Why do I want to be/continue to be a leader?' It is not easy to answer that honestly!

Unhappily contemporary church leaders have not always been aware of the full implication of what they are getting involved in. Unquestionable Christian leadership will make huge inroads into our lives. Better not to respond to the Lord's call to leadership to you unless you are prepared for this. Significant leadership will determine where you live—you are no longer free to pick and choose your location. It will always be seen in relation to the leadership you are exercising. Does living where I do enhance or detract from the leadership I am involved in? Mobility in the United Kingdom seems to be acceptable at almost every other level of life except the christian level. Christian commitment (especially in leadership) is often at the mercy of work, taste, comfort and convenience.

Christian leadership will also determine how you live. The devil is an extremist and will trap us into an extravagance which is justified by the goodness of God or into a poverty which is supposed to enhance a non-materialist, non-acquisitive attitude to life. Plenty or poverty are not the issue. The question to be answered is, 'Does my lifestyle help or hinder those whom I am leading, and is God pleased not only with my inward condition, but also with my outward manifestation of it?' These are deep matters, and much easier to legislate on for others than for ourselves.

Christian leadership will also affect your career prospects. I have seen a number of godly, gifted, excellent leaders lost to us through the pressure of career advancement. It is not always right to commit career suicide on the basis of the call of God upon our lives—but sometimes it is. It does demand strength of character and clarity in hearing the voice of God to know the difference. Few of us are able to do so without very positive and godly input into our lives from others. Many are not open to this and justify career advancement on the basis that Christians need to hold key positions in commerce, industry and the professions. This latter is true, but is not always the real motive for career progress. The enormous pressure to be successful in the world is there from an early age. Proud Christian parents will often speak of their children 'doing well' purely in financial and social terms, rather than their increasing effectiveness as citizens of the kingdom of God.

Future security, in worldly terms, will also be at risk in the call to leadership. Four of the men on our pastoral team at this time have not only committed career suicide, but the future security of themselves and their families has become very vulnerable. One was for more than twenty years a research chemist in industry; another was a chartered accountant for twelve years; yet another flew jet aircraft out of Heathrow Airport in London, and his pilot's licence is now no longer valid; the fourth member of the team was in banking for over twenty years, having reached post-managerial status. In different ways and at different times God laid his hand upon them for leadership in his church, and their response, while realistic and difficult, was ready. There are only two motives that would make a man 'eager to be a church leader' and would sustain him after he has cut his landlines and put out to sea—and these are a deep love for Christ and a genuine concern for his body on earth, the church. Perhaps Paul's poignant encouragement to Timothy is not so out of place today as often it has seemed: 'If a man is eager to be a church leader, he desires an excellent work.' The implications of being or becoming a leader are far-reaching and profound.

God has called us to warfare, and in the day of battle not only must the leaders know where the troops are and what their capability is, but the troops must also know who the leaders are and how well they can be trusted to follow God's strategy and rout the enemy. Inevitably the enemy knows the importance of leadership and will attempt to thwart godly biblical leadership or, if possible, eliminate it altogether and replace God's pattern with a sub-standard alternative which is plausible, attractive, comfortable and useless.

Quite clearly, from the beginning leadership figured prominently in the period of Acts. On returning to Jerusalem after the ascension of Jesus the first thing they attended to was the strengthening of the leadership band of the apostles. The way they did it has caused controversy and comment (Acts 1:23-26), but the fact that they did it is beyond question. Peter gave clear leadership himself in guiding that tiny, vulnerable band of believers to strengthen the leadership 'so then someone must join us' (Acts 1:21). It was not an option, but an obligation.

As the church begins to grow with an awesome rapidity the need for the recognition of and development of leadership quickly emerges. The reason for leadership is clearly seen in Acts 6:1: 'Some time later, as the number of disciples kept growing, there was a quarrel.' There is a romantic preconception that church growth will be so exhilarating and give evidence of the blessing of God that it will be trouble-free. I know of no situation where this has ever been the case. Growth involves conflict—and conflict demands good leadership. God is a God of order, and division, faction, resentment and dissension are antagonistic to the good order of God.

The basis for the quarrel is easy enough to see, but

the consequence was so far reaching that only the wisdom of God given to godly leadership was able to handle it. Even before Jesus came the Jews had begun to spread out from the land they had been given. They dispersed around the Mediterranean and the Roman Empire. Gradually they forgot the language of their fathers and used the Greek language. These were the Hellenists, and when they visited Israel they could no longer speak Hebrew and so went to different synagogues. As in the principality of Wales today there are Welsh-speaking and English-speaking chapels and churches, so in Israel there were Hebrew-speaking and Greek-speaking synagogues. Another factor which opened up the isolation and parochialism of the Jews was that in the synagogues there were three lists of people who attended. The prime list contained those who were Jewish thoroughbreds—born Jews who were faultless in pedigree and ancestry. The second list comprised those who had been Gentiles, but were now converted to the Jewish faith and were baptized Jews. They were Jews in every way—baptized, circumcised, and kept the law—except they were not born Jews. The third list was made up of those who appreciated the worship in the synagogue and valued the high morality and the straightforward monotheism of Judaism. They benefited enormously from the Jews, but never converted to Judaism. These were the 'God-fearers'.

All of this was opening up the exclusiveness of Judaism, and with its growth and development of influence it created problems—there were two different cultures within the same church. The church was in danger in its infancy of dividing into two and creating two denominations. As always, this polarized around a reasonably straightforward and relatively trivial issue, but was pursued with bitterness. How familiar and sad it all is to us in the twentieth century! But the matter was dealt with so ably that we never hear of this problem emerging ever again. Effective leadership was appointed to do this. Some needed to be in charge in order to control the situation and solve the problem.

Luke recalls the two main requirements for leadership here (Acts 6:3). Those who are to be sought must be full of the Holy Spirit. Many of our sore problems in leadership today arise from a neglect of this very first principle. Too many Christian leaders are filled with their own ideas rather than with the Spirit of God. The result is that they speak, decide and act out of their minds and emotions rather than out of an awareness of the guidance or the prohibition of the Spirit of God.

Here clearly the Bible is speaking of spiritual baptism rather than spiritual birth. It is a reference to the event of Pentecost in Acts 2 without which the other twenty-seven chapters do not make sense. It is the reality which God intended to occur at the beginning of our Christian pilgrimage, although the facts of the matter have not always indicated that it is so. It is the continual saturating release of the Spirit within us resulting in the gifts and the fruit of the Holy Spirit being manifested by us. It is the submission of our whole personality to the experience which the Bible describes with two of nature's most destructive elements—wind and fire, resulting in blowing and burning. Indeed the message of Acts is that the only things which last for eternity are the things which God does—the rest is wood, hay and stubble which will disappear.

Secondly leaders are to be full of wisdom—the ability to see things from God's point of view. This is never easy to do, but God does give a very clear promise that 'if any of you lacks wisdom, he should pray to God, who will give it to him; because God gives generously and graciously to all' (Jas 1:5). That is a bold, categorical statement which is easy to proclaim, but very difficult to practise.

Where leadership is filled with the Spirit of God and the wisdom of God, it can be trusted to lead. That happened then, and God intends that it should happen still. For those who are concerned to have good leadership I need to ask: 'What are you looking for in your leaders?' Other qualities and gifts no doubt must take their place, but these without the fullness of the Spirit and wisdom will come to nothing, or worse, will come to grief. For those who are concerned to be good leaders I need to ask: 'Are you filled with the Holy Spirit and the wisdom of God?' If not, then no matter how long your experience or how impressive your gifts you are in serious danger of misleading rather than leading. It is possible to stop right now and in humility and faith to ask the Lord to fill you with both.

The result of such leadership will always be the same to a greater or lesser degree: 'The word of God continued to spread. The number of disciples in Jerusalem grew larger and larger, and a great number of priests accepted the faith.' Good leadership will be effective in extending and enriching the kingdom of God.

Looking back over the years it is difficult to be precise about whose influence has affected me most—I am debtor to so many! I suppose my grandfather with his quiet, unpretentious piety first made a deep and lasting impression on me. To this day I can remember some of his sayings: 'Son,' he would say, 'you can watch a thief but you can never watch a liar!' 'Take your umbrella with you on a dry day, and you will always have it on a wet one!' was his counsel. He was a belt-and-braces man! My parents, too, impressed me with their willingness to work hard, and to be beholden to none. Their quiet contentment with very little and their constant desire to please others rather than themselves persists as a poignant memory. Later life was to bring many others to challenge me and sometimes to change me, for I saw in them what I believed life was about and what my heart yearned after.

In the matter of leadership, however, style and gift and impact may well vary, but the example of Jesus must for ever be our goal. The original leadership in the Acts church had not only personally heard his teaching, but had witnessed him putting it into practice. Having learned it from him and practised it themselves, they were then able to pass on to others the realities of leadership seen in him.

The Acts church was a well-led church. Jesus' most penetrating and unself-conscious description of his leadership is recorded for us in his teaching in John 10. There he describes himself as the good shepherd. Although it is difficult for most of us who have been raised in and continue to live in an urban and industrial society to appreciate the implication and significance of shepherding, it is not completely lost on us when it comes to leadership. In Bible times the shepherd was a concept used of secular leaders, and of course was used of the leaders of God's people (see Num 27; Ezek 34; Jer 23; and Is 40).

There are ten fundamental issues relating to good leadership in John 10. All Christian leadership constantly needs to be lived under the scrutiny of these ten issues. Military, political, commercial and social leadership are markedly different from the leadership which God requires of his leaders. Jesus made a point of emphasizing this to his leaders. 'You know,' he said, 'that the men who are considered rulers of the heathen have power over them, and the leaders have complete authority. This, however, is not the way it is among you. If one of you wants to be great, he must be the servant of the rest; and if one of you wants to be first, he must be the slave of all' (Mk 10:42-44; GNB, adapted). Jesus reverses the values and concepts of men! Greatness in the kingdom of God is not perceived in the number of servants a man has, but in the number of men he serves.

We need a lot of encouragement, not only in facing our motive for leadership, but also in facing up to the meaning of Christian leadership. Let me list what Jesus said a leader must be in order that you may find it easy to check out your own leadership and others may be able to appreciate leadership qualities in you.

1. Every leader is first of all a disciple (Jn 10:1-2)

Great confusion has reigned through failure to appreciate that a leader's *function* is quite distinct from any other form of Christian service, but his *status* is unquestionably the same as any other Christian—he is a sinner saved by grace. 'The man who does not enter the sheep pen by the gate, but climbs in some other way is a thief and a robber. The man who goes in through the gate is the shepherd of the sheep.' The shepherd gets into the fold by the same entrance as the sheep—he is neither ashamed nor afraid, so that he tries to get in by some other route. I take this to mean that the leader enters into the reality of the church's life in Christ in the same way as every other member of the flock. He must embrace the salvation package like everyone else and experience New Testament conversion, which comprises recognizing that in the sight of God he is a sinner; repenting of his sin; receiving Jesus Christ as Lord and Saviour; being baptized in water; being baptized in the Holy Spirit; and becoming a living member of the new body of Christ on earth—the church. This is New Testament conversion, and this is the way the leader must go to enter the sheepfold. How can he lead others into the full reality of New Testament conversion if he has not experienced it himself?

2. Every leader must know his flock personally and intimately (Jn 10:3)

The leader knows the name, history, hopes, fears and dreams of those whom he leads: 'The sheep hear his voice as he calls his own sheep by name.' This is as true of the pastor, Christ's under-shepherd, as it is in its original context where it referred to Christ himself. It takes time and a depth of relationship to be able to distinguish one voice from another. When we moved from Scotland to England, every voice on the telephone was strange. If I wasn't told, I had to ask who was speaking. With the passage of the weeks and months that changed. There were some voices that became all too familiar! But as I related to people and they related to me voices became people—and these were people who were individuals.

With the significant development and growth of a church the sheer logistics make it impossible for the leader to adhere to this principle throughout the whole membership of the church. He must ensure, however, that the principle is made practical by others so that the flock is adequately and properly pastored. His task will change from leading the flock to leading the leaders of the flock. This will not happen immediately, but I have found living through the transitional period extraordinarily difficult practically and deeply frustrating emotionally and spiritually. However, creating smaller 'flocks' within the flock must happen so that effective leadership can be given.

The true leader gets to know those whom he leads well enough to know when to carry them with tenderness and when to prod them out of lethargy. He knows when to encourage the hesitant and when to correct the wayward.

A lady in Glasgow was visited by an official who was acting on behalf of the Census Office. Having asked about the number of rooms in the house and the kind of facilities that were provided, he went on to ask how many people lived there. She responded by saying aloud: 'Well, there's Tom, and Mary, and Isobel and John. . . .' The Census man interrupted by saying: 'Lady, it's not names I want. All I want is numbers.' 'Mister,' she said, 'they may only be numbers to you, but they are all names to me!' For the true leader those whom he leads are all names to him. How well, how intimately, how sensitively do you know those you lead? What steps do you take to ensure that you know them?

3. Every leader must bring the whole flock out of the fold (Jn 10:3-4)

Leadership will not allow the flock to settle for cloistered cosiness or the holy huddle. He will disallow the ghetto mentality which promotes an in-turned, introverted preoccupation with themselves. How much time we spend simply nourishing our own life for its own sake. Bishop Lesslie Newbigin once commented that 'the church is the only society on earth which exists primarily for its non-members'. The New Testament in general and Acts in particular wholeheartedly endorse this. How determinedly we must hold to the reality symbolized by the cross rather than the circle. A circle is circumscribed and exclusive. It draws its boundary lines and gives little encouragement for those within it to venture significantly beyond it and often less encouragement for those outside it to come within it. The cross on the other hand reaches up to heaven and thrusts down to hell and extends its crossbeam like outstretched arms encompassing the whole wide world. The fish may well be the symbolic reminder of the centre of our faith—Jesus Christ. The dove may well be the reminder of the enabler of our faith—the Holy Spirit. But the cross, among other things, will for ever be a reminder to our faith that we have a responsibility to reach up to heaven, to plunder hell and to reach out in the name of Jesus and in the power of the Holy Spirit to touch and minister to the world.

The leader will be responsible for leading the flock out of introspection and into new adventures for God. The word which Jesus used *(ekballo)* is a strong one and brooks little gentleness. It means 'to put forth' in the sense of 'throwing out'. The shepherd will use his strong admonition and teaching invested in his spiritual authority to overcome their objections, quell their fears, stir their lethargy and encourage their hearts.

To be salt in a diseased and decomposing society and light in a darkened world is a simple concept, but a high calling and a sobering challenge.

4. Every leader will lead from the front (Jn 10:3-4)

He will not only *tell,* he will *show.* He will only ask others to do what he himself is prepared to do. There is little validity in exhorting the flock to pray if the exhortation comes from lips that seldom pray. There is limited value in teaching the flock to be wise in financial stewardship if the teacher himself does not honour the Lord properly and honourably with his wealth. There will always be a blunt cutting edge to the encouragement to exercise the gifts of the Holy Spirit if the encourager gives little evidence of freedom and effectiveness in this area himself. It is a dull formalism to issue the call to live by faith when the caller is patently living by sight and substance. The leader should always explore the way ahead and discover new dimensions of spiritual geography to ensure that all is safe and well and good for the flock to join him there.

He should never take his cue from the sheep, nor should he ever be like the fractious sheepdog snapping at their heels. He will always be positive and create initiatives within which his people can move with confidence and expectancy, rather than simply responding to need and reacting to crises.

How much is contained in that directive of Jesus: 'He *leads* them out . . . he goes *ahead* of them.'

5. Every leader is trusted not because of what he says, but because of who he is (Jn 10:4-5)

'The sheep follow him, because they know his voice. They will not follow someone else; instead, they will run away from such a person, because they do not know his voice.' Spiritual sheep instinctively know the voice they can trust. They take notice not so much of what is being said, but who is saying it. I think this is one of the most awesome things about Christian leadership in these days when familiar landmarks are left far behind and new spiritual territory is being explored in the name of Jesus. Often there are few around to be consulted as God continues to do the same thing differently.

It is the charlatan who attempts to exploit this. It is the wise and humble leader who will hesitate as long as is necessary to take his bearings and make sure, as far as he is able, that God is in what he is doing—and will then proceed knowing full well that others will follow. After all, the best definition of a leader is 'someone whom others are following'. How important it is that the leader will be as sure as he possibly can be that his voice is echoing the voice of God.'

6. Every leader will be careful to guard the access to the flock (Jn 10:7,9)

We should never be surprised that savage, marauding wolves (many of them in sheep's clothing—unlikely and surprising people) will attempt to invade the fold and plunder and wound and upset the sheep. By one means or another they will attempt to gain control, exercise influence and dominate the flock. Jesus clearly foresaw that this would happen and warned his people and their leaders so that they would know what to expect. In the twentieth century, as well as in the first century, we have lived to realize the necessity of such a warning.

'I am the gate for the sheep. . . .' Again it is difficult for us to appreciate the full significance of this. The wall of the sheepfold was built up to about three feet, so creating a circle. The circle was broken, however, to create an entrance and an exit. The sheep normally passed into the sheepfold under the shepherd's staff as they entered so that he could inspect them one by one to make sure none was injured. Once they were in, the shepherd himself sat in the gap in the circle. He would build a fire in front of him to keep him warm on the cold night, to cook his food and to scare wild animals away. In this way the flock was safe as long as the shepherd 'plugged' the entrance to the fold. None could get in or out apart from him. The wise leader will always be aware of who has access to his flock—this is not paternalistic, but practical.

Years ago someone from Guatemala had a word from the Lord for me that I was to be extremely careful about who was allowed to minister from our pulpit. I took less notice than I should have done of her warning, and ultimately paid the price for my carelessness. It was soon after that a trusted colleague of mine in another pastorate discovered he had a visitor from overseas on his hands, and felt he could not reasonably use him enough. He phoned me and asked if I would allow him to preach at our evening service. The time was short and my friend sounded anxious, if not even desperate, and I agreed—after a bit of persuasion—because our own programme was already under way and I still had the warning in my mind which came via the lady from Guatemala. It took us nine months to recover from that evening service! The flock was hurt—and I was to blame. I have never forgotten the experience, and I think I have learned a cardinal lesson on leadership. No matter how harmless it seems, no matter how pressurized the situation, be careful to guard the access to the flock!

Sometimes we have to guard not simply against people, but against wrong ideas and emphases which come flooding in through books and tapes. The flock is not helped by these and often its development is hindered by our failure to be careful.

7. Every leader is unafraid of confrontation (Jn 10:12-13)

The hired man, the professional who has little interest in the flock apart from earning his living, or the person for whom leadership is a hobby or one interest among many others, will shrink from the disagreeable and unpleasant encounters with those who would 'snatch the sheep and scatter them'. Confronting difficulty and danger will always be a part of Christian leadership. It will inevitably lead to criticism, misunderstanding, and maybe even worse. It may well cause sleepless nights and tears. It will result in being emotionally drained and pressurize you to the point where you want to resign, retire or even die. When the going is tough through fierce confrontation, a lethal heart-attack seems preferable to continuing the struggle.

The strong counsel of Jesus is that it shall not be so with you. You are a leader under God and your task is to remain there and fight for the flock. A wise leader keeps his head when everyone around him is losing theirs. Enemies don't tend to be attracted to emaciated, scrawny sheep. They are attracted to a large flock of well-fed specimens who bear witness to good nourishment in good pastures and beside still waters, well-exercised and able to reproduce themselves in a remarkable way. The more evidence there is of the blessing of God among the flock, the more likely is the enemy to take notice and make his move to steal what doesn't belong to him.

8. Every leader has a vision for the sheep in his flock (Jn 10:9)

'Whoever comes in by me will be saved; he will come in and go out and find pasture.' Salvation is never an end in itself. It is a means to an end—and that end is to please God. The shepherd does not nourish and care for the sheep for their own sake, but because he has an end in view for them. Almost all the sheep around Jerusalem were destined for sacrifice.

In AD 65 Cestius, the governor of Palestine, had difficulty in persuading the Emperor Nero of the immense importance of the Jewish religion in any attempt to govern the area. The Jewish historian Josephus tells us that in order to impress Nero, he asked the High Priest to take a census of the lambs killed for the Passover in one year. According to Josephus the number was 256,500. The law said there would be a minimum party of ten people to one lamb. It meant that there would be a minimum number of pilgrims to the Passover of 2,565,000. However, a quarter of a million lambs had to be roasted over an open fire on a spit of pomegranate wood. These lambs came from the surrounding countryside.

What God is looking for is lives that will be wholly surrendered to him. Real worship always involves the participation of a body. In the Old Testament it was a dead body that was required—presumably to symbolize a living body. But in the New Testament a living body is required. 'So then, my brothers,' cries Paul to the Christians in Rome, 'because of God's great mercy to us I appeal to you: offer yourselves as a living sacrifice to God, dedicated to his service and pleasing to him. This is the true worship that you should offer.' The leader is concerned to nourish the flock so that they can be offered as living, effective sacrifices to God.

9. Every leader cares for his flock at personal cost (Jn 10:11)

'I am the good shepherd, who is willing to die for the sheep.' Leadership will make enormous demands on our time. So much so that some will no longer be able to earn their living in the secular world. It is not always right that Christian leadership is dismissed in such circumstances. Sometimes, not always, it is the familiar, accepted and secure pattern of earning a living that has to go in order that good leadership can be maintained.

The leader's privacy will frequently be invaded. He needs his sabbath like everyone else, and will need with regularity to withdraw from the heavy pressures and exciting possibilities of leadership in order to recharge his batteries not just spiritually, but emotionally and mentally too. Yet his right to a life of his own has gone for ever. Frustrating and wearying this may be, but the price needs to be paid. Emotional energy will be drained from him in his leadership task, sometimes leaving little for his marriage and his family. Unless this is recognized and watched, he will pay a heavier price in this area than God requires. How faithfully we need to pray for our leaders as they work to fulfil the task that God has given them in the power of the Holy Spirit and under the protection of the blood of Jesus Christ. Unless we do so he will be prone to fulfil his task grudgingly rather than gladly and his leadership will easily degenerate into leading by enforcement rather than by example. No doubt it was because of his awareness of these dangers that Peter writes so movingly:

> I appeal to you to be shepherds of the flock God gave you and to take care of it willingly, as God wants you to, and not unwillingly. Do your work, not for mere pay, but from a real desire to serve. Do not try to rule over those who have been put in your care, but be examples to the flock. And when the Chief Shepherd appears you will receive the glorious crown which will never lose its brightness (1 Pet 5:2-3, GNB, adapted).

10. Every leader will be concerned for the whole flock of God (Jn 10:16)

'There are other sheep which belong to me that are not in this sheep pen. I must bring them, too; they will listen to my voice, and they will become one flock with one shepherd.' In context Jesus envisages the coming in of the Gentiles and the restoration of Israel. But the principle remains in our day. How easy it is with the activity and the variety and the pressure of church life to be exclusive and insular and isolationist and limited. To widen the horizons is disturbing and to extend the borders beyond our traditions and prejudices is acutely uncomfortable. John Wesley's greeting, 'Is your heart as my heart? Give me your hand!' may make interesting reading, but surely it is difficult in practice. The good leader will want, without any compromise, to embrace and encourage all who own Jesus Christ as absolute Lord and only Saviour.

The early church in Acts moved with power that had clear direction and control. Surely Peter and the rest had learned well from the teaching of their Master and taught others how to lead from his principles and example.

5
Look, God Did It!

Just over two years ago someone said to me with great authority and finality, 'You realize, don't you, that the charismatic movement is finished!' I was surprised by his assurance and inquisitive about his motive for saying it to me. However, I did realize that my life and service for the Lord is far too short to be involved in a movement—charismatic or otherwise. The only thing which drives me relentlessly on is that while life lasts I might discover the beating heart of basic New Testament Christianity, experience it in my own life, and then lead others into its reality with confidence, expectancy, joy and gratitude.

One evening in our church the whole tone of the service was low-key with gentle, unremarkable worship and true but unspectacular preaching. As we moved towards its conclusion there were some words of knowledge (see 1 Corinthians 12:8). Among these was the indication that a woman was in the congregation with an extremely painful, stiff and swollen knee. She, among others, came forward for prayer and sat in the front row of the centre section of the church. I, along with another, received her. There was nothing planned about this—she was simply sitting there waiting to be prayed for. We had never seen her before. She was elderly, had been a Christian for less than two weeks, was wearing a light blue trouser-suit and her knee was extremely painful, stiff and swollen—so much so that one leg of her trousers was absolutely taut around the knee.

We prayed and asked her from time to time how her knee was responding. She felt heat in it; then increased, painless movement; and then startled us by comparing one knee with the other in some concern since the affected knee had become smaller than the knee which caused her no trouble. 'Look, God did it!' she exclaimed. Indeed, he did—there could be no other explanation! Others along the front of the congregation were experiencing similar touches from the Lord. The daughter of this lady, who came with her to the front, was beautifully restored in a deep relationship with her mother, and her son, who had been watching all this going on from the gallery, joined us at the front and he too was beautifully united with his mother and grandmother. It was moving to see it all happen at the front of our church—and God did it.

This is normal New Testament Christianity. We have lived with abnormal Christianity for such a long time that we call what we have lived with normal, and so when we begin to touch God's normal we are prone to call it abnormal. We live in a world that is impressed by the spectacular and the sensational. A man who can bend spoons without touching them attracts an astounded press, and a man who can leap over many London double-decker buses on a motorbike excites a ghoulish interest, but a man who can change and transform human lives and make them whole is despised and dismissed. But Jesus Christ is in that business and continues to exercise his power and authority through his body on earth, the church. Although we have reneged largely on our original calling under God, he is calling us again, not so much to the spectacular and the sensational, but to spiritual life and reality which transform lives and make men whole. It is to a word declared, but also to a word demonstrated that God calls us.

'Miracle' is a great word with a very loose use. Thomas Hardy, for example, would not allow a telephone to be installed in his home for many years and when at last he did, he would very seldom use it. He regarded it as an uncanny miracle! I remember watching a Scottish Cup Final football match at Hampden Park in Glasgow when Greenock Morton were playing. Their goalkeeper, a man called Jimmy Cowan, had an extraordinary save. The ball actually was past him and he leapt back and scooped it off the goal-line in a fraction of a second. It was described everywhere the next day in the banner headlines of the newspapers as a miracle save! As young people come close to an examination and as all the horror of ignorance dawns and time runs out many of them say, 'It will be a miracle if I pass!'

Miracle and knowledge—or lack of it—are often linked. A Roman sailor would have regarded it either as a myth or a miracle if you had told him that one day a ship measuring more than a thousand feet in length and weighing more than 80,000 tons would sail the oceans. Even in my lifetime there was a day when an aeroplane flying at twice the speed of sound would have been described as a miracle.

We need to put some content into the word before we use it in the context of the Acts of the Apostles and the contemporary church. The word 'miracle' comes from the Latin verb *mirari,* which means 'to wonder'. But to be filled with wonder does not constitute a miracle. When I hear a young woman in our congregation speak in fluent Russian—although she is one of the finest primary school teachers I have known—I am filled with wonder! I could never do that! When I hear Roy Castle, another member of our church, play some musical instruments (particularly the trumpet!) I am filled with wonder. I could certainly never do that! Yet neither of these instances constitutes a miracle. There is more to a miracle than being filled with wonder. We need to give much more content to a miracle. An old teacher of mine has defined a miracle as something which defies human skill to perform and baffles human wisdom to explain. That is good, but it is not good enough, and we need to widen the concept still further.

In Acts the word *teras* (*terata*, plural) is used nine times. It refers to something strange which is occurring, causing the person observing to marvel and be filled with wonder. It describes a happening which appeals to the imagination. Generally however, it occurs with the word *semeia* (*semeion*, singular) which means 'a sign' which is intended to appeal to the understanding. This latter word is used of the miracles of Jesus sometimes. A third word is used for 'miracle' in the New Testament—*dunameis* (*dunamis*, singular). This is the word from which we get our words 'dynamic', 'dynamite' and 'dynamo'. It has the concept of 'power' in it. In a miracle there is power. Indeed a miracle might well be defined as an event in which God's power has made a special entry into our lives. Before Jesus came there were men and women who were beyond human help. Jesus brought to their needs a power which no one else had. This was why the disciples were so crestfallen and anxious when Jesus kept indicating to them that he was going to leave them. Before he came all they could offer people was a listening ear and sympathy. When he was with them they had power to meet their needs as well as sympathy to enter in to how they felt. Now that he was going from them, they feared they would be back to square one again—with nothing but sympathy to offer. *Dunamis,* however, is used of works of a supernatural origin and character which could not be produced by natural agents or means.

A 'sign' *semeia, semeion* not only staggered men with sheer wonder, however, but showed them something. It showed the character, nature and heart of God. Power *(dunamis)* is a neutral thing—it can help or save, but it can also kill or destroy. Atomic power is a good example of this. There are enormous social and industrial benefits from atomic power, but there are also awesome military and political implications caused by it. You can tell a great deal about a person—or a nation for that matter—by the way he uses power of any kind. The power of God in the gospels was used to heal the sick, feed the hungry, bring joy and hope to the mourner, and rescue and give reassurance to the fearful. In a miracle not only is man caused to stagger in wonder and amazement, but the love, grace, goodness and majesty of God is seen. A miracle displays God's power, but at the same time demonstrates God's character.

A miracle is really three things at once—a natural event in that it takes place within the sphere of the natural world; an unnatural event in that it cuts across the normal, natural process of nature; and a supernatural event in that its source or origin comes from outside nature itself. A working definition of a miracle, then, is that it is a natural event which follows an unnatural course and has a supernatural cause or origin.

The Acts of the Apostles contains many such occurrences in its unfolding history of the triumphant, though painful and demanding spreading of the gospel from Jerusalem to Rome in one generation. The gospel in Acts is not only declared, but also demonstrated.

The appeal of the early church was not only to the ears, but also to the eyes. God moved in inexplicable power, and society was left asking how what they saw could have occurred. Again and again these early Christians were responsible for declaring to them the reason and source of these supernatural events—the Jesus of Nazareth whom they had crucified was not dead as they supposed, but was alive, and it was through his power that they were able to do what they were doing. Resurrection was not simply an historical fact which needed to be grasped, it was a contemporary reality whose evidence was before them. This is the Golden Age of the church. This is the church as God meant it to be.

For too long the church in our day has relied on appealing to only one sense in man—his hearing. There is an urgent need to appeal to a second sense—his seeing. We live in a world which has become word-proof. So many words bombard us from so many different sources. Men pay little heed to the vast majority of them. They are simply background sounds in a very noisy world. The eyes will need to be arrested before the ears will listen.

The greatest miracle of all that underlies almost every page of Acts is the miracle of the salvation of men whose lives were profoundly changed by the grace of God and infused by the power of the Holy Spirit. There are countless evidences of this inherent in the history of the first generation of the church. Most of these transformations we will know nothing about until at last we all get to heaven and are able to share how God met us and what happened afterwards. On the first day of the church's life—her birthday—there were 3,000 people born again (Acts 2:41). That happened in Jerusalem, and the Jerusalem church, which began at Pentecost with 3,120, sustained its growth and development in an extraordinary way. Luke tells us (Acts 21:20) that when

Paul returned to the Jerusalem church towards the end of his remarkable ministry among the Gentiles he was invited by the elders of the church to look around him and 'see how many thousands of Jews have become believers. . . '. The word for 'thousands' there is *muriades* which really means multiples of ten thousand. The event of Pentecost cannot be regarded as an isolated incident in the church's life, but rather the beginning of an ongoing romance of faith in the power of the Holy Spirit. This was only the Jerusalem church, but there were other locations—in some cases whole communities—where salvation had been witnessed as an indisputable reality.

Few individual incidents of this are given, but one is the story which has excited many imaginations and stimulated many hearts to yearn for God. Perhaps it is because of his strategic ministry which is to follow, but the Holy Spirit caused Luke to record in some detail the conversion of Saul of Tarsus—not only the event itself, but Paul (as he is afterwards called) retelling the event in defence of himself before others. Here is the record of a man who was an enemy of Christians changed into their friend—one who had been an aggressive opponent was now an eager advocate of all that the church was and stood for. He is described in an historical novel by an Asian Christian written some time during the middle of the second century as 'A man of little stature, thin-haired upon the head, crooked in the legs, of good state of body, with eyebrows meeting, and nose somewhat hooked, full of grace; for sometimes he appeared like a man and sometimes he had the face of an angel.'[9]

Whatever his appearance, this was the man God was going to use to bring the gospel to the Gentiles; to write half the New Testament; to put down on paper the implication of Jesus' life on the basis of the information we have in the four gospels. He was the first and only writer in the Bible to state the gospel in a straightforward way. St Augustine's life was transformed as he read Romans 3. Romans 5 was the channel God used to reach Martin Luther and Romans 8 to touch John Wesley one Wednesday evening in 1738. He wrote in his journal, 'I felt my heart strangely warmed. I felt I did trust in Christ, Christ alone, for salvation: and an assurance was given me that He had taken away my sins, even mine, and saved me from the law of sin and death.'[10] One miracle has followed another as a result of God transforming the life of Saul of Tarsus.

He was a man who was well provided for materially, since he was a Roman citizen and so must have been a man of considerable means. He was well endowed mentally, sharpening and disciplining his mind at the University of Tarsus—a Greek city whose university provided a wealth of art, music, drama and culture. He also studied at the University of Jerusalem and sat at the feet of his teacher Gamaliel. Morally, Saul of Tarsus had a long and impressive ancestry. It caused him to be proud of what he was by birth and he sought to maintain his heritage in life. He was determined with his ambitious, assured, iron will to get to heaven as a result of his own goodness.

It was there on the Damascus Road (Acts 9) about 150 miles from Jerusalem, on his way to persecute Christian men and women, that God met him and totally changed him.

Saul's conversion is a strong reminder that conversion is always personal. Often through the years people have said to me, 'I didn't have a Damascus Road experience!' On the face of it this is a silly and quite unnecessary statement since it presupposes that there is some kind of classified confrontation with Christ. It is as if what happened to Saul of Tarsus was a 'grade A' conversion! I certainly did not have a Damascus Road experience. But then Saul did not have a Hebron Hall experience, where the building was seven-eighths empty and a forgotten preacher was preaching on the life of Joseph. That was the place and the occasion of my encounter with Christ. There are features of Saul's conversion which are unknown to me, but then there are features of my conversion which are unknown to him! The important thing is not where I met Christ or how, but that I really did and that he changed my life. This is the most basic and profound miracle in human experience. Saul's conversion is marvellous, but it is not typical in its detail—only in its reality.

Saul's conversion is equally a reminder that conversion is normally a process. It was not sudden, as has often been supposed. Very few conversions are as sudden as they may seem at first sight. Much later, when Saul of Tarsus, now become Paul the Apostle, is giving his defence before King Agrippa, he recalled how the risen Christ had spoken to him clearly on the Damascus Road and said (Acts 26:14): 'You are hurting yourself by hitting back, like an ox kicking against its owner's stick.' Before that dramatic miracle-crisis on the Damascus Road there had been a time of considerable preparation. Almost certainly Saul had seen Jesus Christ alive in the flesh—he was in Jerusalem at the time of Jesus' death and resurrection. It is impossible to assess the profound impact this must have had. He must have been deeply affected too by many Christians who were serene and bold as he committed them to prison. But perhaps the most powerful influence of all on Saul's pre-Christian life was the event of the martyrdom of Stephen (Acts 7:57-8:1). Stephen had spent the time just prior to his death taking his judges systematically through the Old Testament. Stephen had clearly said (Acts 7) that you cannot lock God up in a building, nor can you restrict him to the Holy Land, for he had appeared to Moses and Abraham outside Israel and transformed their lives and deeply affected the lives of God's own people as a result.

So Jesus met this able, ambitious, good man and changed him. He had to step outside the Holy Land for it to happen—and often we have to be on unfamiliar territory where our prejudices and our traditions can be roundly confronted for it to happen to us. He had to recognize who Jesus was and respond to what Jesus said in order for his life to be changed—and so it is with us. This great man, striding ahead in the mid-day sun, was struck blind before God and became groping, disorientated and as helpless as a little child. God blinded him to enable him to see. Often some see who are blind, while others are blind, but see clearly. God used an unknown church member (Acts 9:10) to minister healing and the baptism of the Holy Spirit to him—and so a new church member was born.

The church will make little progress until it recognizes that all its members need to experience the miracle of salvation—different in detail from that of Saul of Tarsus, but always as real, if not always so dramatic.

Saul is a good example, however, of the necessity not only of being born of the Spirit (in his case on the Damascus Road), but also of being baptized in the Spirit (in his case at the house of Judas in Straight Street, Damascus). Both realities are intended to be part of the conversion experience—in Saul's case separated by a few days, but this is not always necessarily so. The important thing is not, however, when, where or how it happens—but simply that it does. Controversy has raged over this, but the necessity remains. I need not only to be spiritually born, but I need to be spiritually baptized so that I not only become a

Christian, but so that I can continue to be one who is relevant.

The Acts of the Apostles bears eloquent witness to the necessity for Christians to be baptized in the Holy Spirit (see Acts 2; 9; 10; 11; 19). In fact if you remove Acts 2, then the other twenty-seven chapters do not make sense. Someone has said that the Acts of the Apostles would more appropriately be called the Acts of the Holy Spirit. As we mentioned before, the gospel of Luke records all that Jesus *began* to do, whereas the Acts of the Apostles records all that Jesus *continued* to do through his followers, whose lives were now filled with the Holy Spirit. The baptism in the Spirit did not come at the end, but at the beginning of their mission—to enable them to be relevant citizens of the kingdom of God on earth. These early Christians did not hold conferences on evangelism or training programmes on strategy for mission. They were exposed to the fullness of God, described by two of nature's most destructive elements—wind and fire. They experienced the blowing and the burning of the Holy Spirit and so could never be satisfied with anything less than him ever again. The Acts story is unintelligible apart from this reality of the fullness of the Holy Spirit. How eagerly we need to recapture this within the contemporary church. Revival will come, not when the churches are filled with people, but when people are filled with the Holy Spirit.

Whether it is the 120 attending a ten-day prayer meeting at Jerusalem or an ineffective house group of twelve Christian men at Ephesus, the reality of the fullness of the Holy Spirit needs to be experienced. Apollos had taken this Ephesian group as far as he had gone himself and undoubtedly they were disciples (Acts 19:1). Both in Luke and in Acts 'disciples' were always followers of Jesus. These twelve in Ephesus had got as far as the twelve apostles (or indeed the other 108) had got before Pentecost. Clearly, however, Paul's question (Acts 19:2) implies that he observed something was lacking. His question was not so much theological as it was practical: 'Did you receive the Holy Spirit when you became believers?' It may well be that birth and baptism ought to happen together, but they do not always! He was not asking: 'Did the Holy Spirit take up *residence* in your heart when you believed?' But he was asking: 'Did the Holy Spirit pour out his *power* upon you when you believed? Did you have a manifestation of the power of the Holy Spirit when you believed in Jesus?' If the answer to that question is 'Yes' then there is another question to be asked and answered: 'What has happened and where has it all gone, then?'

Their answer is significant. It is often rendered, 'We have not even heard that there is a Holy Spirit,' and this is taken to mean that they were totally ignorant of the Holy Spirit. Manifestly it cannot mean that, since John the Baptist, to whom they refer, consistently taught that if God's people were going to go on with God they needed to get to know the two other persons in the Godhead—the Son of God and the Spirit of God (Jn 1:30, 33). Obviously anyone baptized in water by John the Baptist on the basis of their repentance would be looking for something more. Actually the literal response of the Ephesians is: 'We have not heard that Holy Spirit is.' They are not confessing their ignorance of the Holy Spirit, but rather their ignorance that what John promised has now happened. They had entered into the reality of the faithfulness of God the Father and the forgiveness of God the Son, but had no experience of God the Holy Spirit. These twelve had repented of sin and recognized and received Jesus Christ as their Lord and Saviour—they now needed to know the overwhelming power and the enabling of the Holy Spirit.

If belief in Jesus and baptism in the Holy Spirit are synonymous (and the latter happens automatically as a consequence of the former) then Acts 19:6 is a mystery. Paul ought to have finished with them at the end of Acts 19:5. If he had asked the original question (Acts 19:2) at the end of Acts 19:5 these twelve Ephesian Christians would still have had to answer, 'No!' So Paul says, 'I am going to pray for you now!'

In the next few moments three things happened—Paul placed his hands on them; the Holy Spirit came *upon* them (not *into* them); and all twelve men began to overflow. Often in human experience the mouth is the place where overflow occurs—whether it is the overflow of joy or excitement or relief or gratitude or sadness. It is not because they became mature or perfect at that time, but because they became complete.

Our little grand-daughter was born one Easter Monday. I expect we shall have other grandchildren, but the first will always remain specially memorable—I suppose because it is the impact of a completely new experience for the very first time. We saw her about two hours after her birth in St Thomas' Hospital in London. Our first concern was that both the baby and her mother were fit and well. What we wanted to know about the baby was in effect, 'Are all her parts there and does she function properly?' When a baby is born a mother wants to be sure that it is complete and is functioning as normally as possible after the trauma of birth,—and so do grandparents! So it is too with spiritual birth. There needs to be a godly anxiety which is concerned to ensure that the new spiritual baby is complete and has all it needs for proper development—otherwise growth and progress will not be as God has planned.

I suspect that if Paul were to visit many of our

churches and assemblies and fellowships today he would have to ask a similar question to the one asked of the Ephesian house group—'Did you receive the Holy Spirit when you became believers?' He would discover there is little real evidence of a supernatural dimension among us—little that cannot be understood in terms of us rather than in terms of God! It is unlikely that he would say of many of us, 'You are the sort of Christians I am used to—the kind we knew in the days of the New Testament.' There is a dimension of God that is lacking in practice if not always in theology and preaching today. It must surely be time that we took this seriously. What is there among us both personally and corporately which can only be explained in terms of God?

I think we need to ask ourselves the question: 'What would I reply if he asked me?' This is not in the first instance a theological question, but a practical one. I need to review my way of life and the evidence of his life in me, so that I not only have the security of knowing that I am a pardoned sinner, but that I am also a powerful servant of the Lord—making a relevant and significant impact within the sphere of my calling in God, whether it is constantly in public view or in a more private context. It is not sufficient to settle for a routine, humdrum, lack-lustre mediocrity which achieves so very little and satisfies hardly at all, when all the time there is richness and bounty and fullness as part of our inheritance in Christ.

One of the undeniable features of the life of the early church was that 'many miracles and wonders were being done through the apostles, and everyone was filled with awe' (Acts 2:43). Clearly this was not an isolated incident, but the normal, ongoing and expected feature of Christian living. In the routine expression of Christian living—'at three o'clock in the afternoon, the hour for prayer'—Peter and John are confronted by a man with forty years of the same disease behind him. So this was no superficial, peripheral condition—it was a chronic and apparently irreversible disease from which he was suffering. His problem was not only difficult, but also very public. He was well-known by the community. Peter and John's reaction is impressive because of its simplicity and confidence—'I give you what I have.' These six words are a summary of the church's life in the Acts of the Apostles. There is clearly an extraordinary openness to receive all that God wants to give and an unusual willingness to give what has been received. Such is the secret of a healthy and effective Christian life.

Often we are impotent in the face of the challenges of life because neither individually nor corporately have we waited on God to receive what he wants to give, or else, having received, we want to hang on to what God has so graciously and generously given for ourselves. So the church has become irrelevant within our Western society rather than indispensable. We have forsaken our relevance and effectiveness for five substitutes to dependent faith.

1. Materialism

God has provided material things for us to enjoy—and in itself the material world is the loving and lavish provision of God. However, by sleight of hand the devil has corrupted the good by causing it to blind our eyes to the best. Unconsciously we have often settled for the fact that material things are an end in themselves to be relentlessly pursued for their own sake rather than as a means to an end. In the East the dominating features of society are Communism and Islam, while in the West the ruling force which will ultimately destroy us, if unchecked, is materialism.

2. Activism

The cult of self-effort has never been very far beneath the surface of both ancient and modern man. We respond quickly to achieving by doing rather than by trusting. It is never easy for us to settle for the reality that Christianity begins not with a big 'do', but with a complete and categorical 'done'. As it begins, so it intends to continue. This is not an invitation to indolence, but it is a demand to recognize that it is God who is at work in us, expressing his life and fulfilling his purpose. This is the heart-land of the gospel of Jesus Christ. Humility is not expressed in the things we do for Christ, but in the things we allow him to do for us and then through us.

3. Humanism

The centre of spiritual gravity has shifted from God to man. God—if he exists at all—is there because of man rather than the reverse of that. Man has assumed the central position and all things—including God—exist for his benefit. One fundamental practical result of this is that we become accustomed to think as other men think and give little attention to how God thinks about life in general and our situation in particular. This is a dominating spirit of the age and has entered powerfully into the life of the church. We constantly tend to do God's things in our way. The fact that it doesn't work seems to cut little ice with us, so great is our infatuation with ourselves.

4. Intellectualism

This is an inevitable consequence of dominating humanism. Our understanding and experience for ever become much more dependable criteria for doing or not doing things than the revealed word of God. Only eternity will reveal how often our minds have determined our behaviour rather than Scripture. There is a basic unwillingness to obey if the way of obedience runs counter to our experience and our accumulated wisdom. So we allow the word of God to be shaped by our minds rather than allowing our minds to be shaped by the word of God. This has inescapably led to the greatest tragedy of twentieth century Christianity in the West—we have restricted our experience and expression of Christian faith to the possible. We have a doctrine of the supernatural, but little or no experience to match it.

5. Negativism

Oscar Wilde once said: 'In the English Church a man succeeds not through his capacity for belief, but through his capacity for disbelief. Ours is the only Church where the sceptic stands at the altar, and where St Thomas is regarded as the ideal apostle.'

Pessimism is equated with maturity and spirituality, and hope—that foundation stone of our faith—is condemned to spiritual obscurity. In spite of the fact that one-fifth of the gospels is devoted to Jesus' healing ministry and the discussion occasioned by it; in spite of the fact that there are forty-one distinct instances of healings recorded in the four gospels, absorbing 727 of their 3,779 verses; in spite of all that, as we have seen, we still have faith for sickness rather than for healing so very often. An attitude has clearly formed in the church today which expects nothing from God and so attempts nothing for him.

In spite of social and political persecution the early followers of Christ were much more intent on the demonstration of the word which they proclaimed than they were on their own safety. When Peter and John were eventually released from gaol they met the believers for prayer and delighted themselves with a big view of God and asked for two things. They wanted to be able to continue to speak God's message: 'Allow us, your servants, to speak your message with boldness' (Acts 4:29)—and also to see God's miracles: 'Reach out your hand to heal, and grant that wonders and miracles may be performed through the name of your holy servant Jesus' (Acts 4:30). Little did they expect that God would show himself in power inside the church first of all in answer to their prayers. This is the first time in Acts that the word *church* appears (Acts 5:11). It is an awesome reminder that God is looking for a church which is holy. Hypocrisy and deception are so destructive to the essential fabric of the church that God removes both Ananias and Sapphira to glory rather than allow them to remain and be a cause of humiliating and hurting the new, young, vulnerable body of Christ on earth. The church has much more to fear from corruption within than from opposition from without.

Asking and expecting God to move in power as he desires will result in judgement as well as in blessing, and in surgery as well as in salvation. After all, the very first miracle that Paul was involved in resulted in a man who could see being made blind (Acts 13:11). It will result also in us being confronted by the inscrutable sovereignty of God.

We have discussed the release of Peter from prison (Acts 12:6-19)—and rightly so, since it is an extraordinary phenomenon—but we have given scant attention to the beginning of that chapter and the martyrdom of James. Martyrdom too is part of the ongoing, unfolding life of the new-born church. Undoubtedly

Peter would have followed James to a martyr's grave then had it not been for divine intervention after the Festival of Unleavened Bread. Why did God allow James to die and at the same time cause Peter to live through the now well-known miraculous intervention? It is never easy for us to grasp that God has a different pattern for everyone's life, but we will never be free from being troubled over things we do not understand until we do. As the result of the miracle of Peter's release, however, mothers lost their sons, wives lost their husbands and children their fathers (Acts 12:19). Miracles in human terms can be costly. It was not long, however, before the judgement of God fell on a line of kings and removed them from history altogether (Acts 12:21-23). This Herod's grandfather had perpetrated the 'slaughter of the Innocents'. His uncle had beheaded John the Baptist. Another member of the family dressed Jesus up in his cast-off clothes and laughed at him. This Herod—extravagant, immoral, luxury-loving friend of the Emperor Caligula—despised God, and enough was enough!

The key issue in Acts is that 'meanwhile the word of God continued to spread and grow'. Undoubtedly an integral part of this was the constantly occurring natural events which took an unnatural course and had a supernatural cause or origin. Confronted by the pagan mixture of materialism, rationalism and occultism, people needed a demonstration of the supernatural power of Christ. In almost every chapter of Acts there is some manifestation of the Spirit of Christ—tongues, healings, prophecies, visions, judgements, exorcism, miracles—all of which are evidences of the living God, and help people in a powerful way to come to a living faith in him. It is precisely because of such a free and powerful demonstration of the Spirit of God that 'more and more people were added to the group—a crowd of men and women who believed in the Lord' (Acts 5:14).

In our day the climate in which the contemporary church has to live and serve is astonishingly similar to that facing the early church. True though it may be that we wrestle with the new and bewildering problems created by the revolution of technology—apathy, materialism, the permissive society, the fascination of the occult—the quest for meaning and significance and freedom and forgiveness and hope remain the same in this age as in that. Similar means to communicate the reality of the word we preach are required if we are not to fail and be cast aside as irrelevant.

Not long ago God spoke into our crowded evening congregation by means of the gift of tongues. We then waited quietly for God to give us an interpretation and so an understanding of what had been said in a language that none of us had learned. He did! Although the content of that service was the completing of a series of teachings we had been doing on Family Life, at the end of it someone came to Christ and was born again as a result of that tongue and interpretation. As that new Christian was born all we could do was to stand back in wonder and say: 'Look, God did it!'

6

You Change—I Can't!

Once an admiral was sailing on his flagship on the North Sea. He had left his quarters and gone onto the bridge after darkness had fallen. He looked ahead into the night with his binoculars and to his alarm he saw a light coming directly towards them—they were on a collision course! He gave an order: 'Send a signal; change two degrees south!' Back came the reply: 'You change two degrees north!' Somewhat roused by this blatant flouting of his authority he demanded that another signal should be sent: 'I am an admiral—change two degrees south!' The reply came: 'I am an Able Seaman—you change course two degrees north!' Identity had been revealed and authority had been defied and the admiral knew he was on a collision course not just physically, but also professionally. There was only one course open—the imperious demand. 'I am a battleship and I order you to change course two degrees south!' Back came the irresistible demand: 'I am a lighthouse—you change two degrees north. You change! I can't!'

I heard that story told by Leighton Ford at Spring Harvest—a remarkable festival which continues to grow and become more and more significant in the spiritual life of this country. It is a festival which has become known for its vibrant worship, but its main emphasis is on teaching the word of God and applying it firmly and practically to a wide variety of issues which confront men and women both in society generally and in the church particularly. The whole thrust of these weeks together is based on the fact that the word of God does not, and cannot, change. It is unrealistic to believe that we can defy it, because the reality is that it defies us. It is not the word of God that changes, no matter how pressing the circumstances or deep the desires—it is we who must change, regardless of the position we may hold or the pressure we are under. There is great security in this. It is an unchanging landmark from which we take our bearings and by which we can plot our course on the journey of life.

On page after page in the Acts of the Apostles there is a strong emphasis on the strategic importance of the word of God—both inside as well as outside the church. This was a keynote of the church's life. Within a few days of the ascension of Jesus, Peter was already taking his pastoral role seriously and giving direction to the 120 believers from the book of Psalms (Acts 1:20). The church's new converts spent their time 'learning from the apostles' (Acts 2:42). The teaching which they were giving was biblical, and Luke frequently refers to this priority task in the early church. The Greek verb 'to teach' *(didaskein)* occurs many times in the unfolding record—see Acts 4:2,8; 5:21, 25, 28, 42; 13:12; 15:35; 17:19; 18:11; 20:20; 28:31, etc.

In fact Paul reminds the leaders of the church in Ephesus that he 'did not hold back anything that would be of help to you as I preached and taught in public and in your homes' (Acts 20:20). Later, in that same experience so filled with pathos, he says: 'For I have not held back from announcing to you the whole purpose of God' (Acts 20:27). The word he uses there—*hupostellein* — is sometimes used in nautical circles for pulling down a sail. It is so easy because of our fear of men or our uncertainty about how it will be received to pull down the sails and hold back and shrink from certain aspects of the whole purpose of God that might be unpopular or unfashionable in either secular or religious circles. But with the wind of the Spirit blowing strongly, the apostles refused to pull down their sails in their faithful teaching of the word of God.

So powerfully and manifestly was this the case that even in the earliest days of the church's life the High Priest observed with horror to the Council of the Jewish elders when it was in full session that the apostles had 'spread their teaching all over Jerusalem . . .' (Acts 5:28). So crucial was this to the ongoing life of the church that when it was in danger of being threatened by some of the inevitable pressures of growth the apostles took some very practical steps in appointing others to take responsibility for matters which were encroaching on this priority in their lives. It demanded that the whole church was made aware of the pastoral and practical need which endangered the fundamental ministry of the apostles. They were very forthright about the tension they faced: 'It is not right for us to neglect the preaching of God's word in order to handle finances.' So deacons were brought into being and the apostles were released to 'give our full time to prayer and the work of preaching' (Acts 6:1-7).

This was a key part of the early church's history. Other things—legitimate, good and necessary things, often—have come in to take the place of sharing the word of God in its totality with the people of God. I sense that often there is a loss of confidence in preaching and teaching the word of God in today's church. In many ways this is an undramatic and unspectacular aspect of church life—yet we minimize it, substitute other things for it, and even neglect it at our peril.

Paul and Barnabas spent a long time in Iconium 'speaking boldly about the Lord' (Acts 14:3). Paul spent eighteen months teaching the word of God in Corinth (Acts 18:11). Most impressive, however, of all the records is at Ephesus where 'Paul went into the synagogue and for three months spoke boldly with the people, holding discussions with them and trying to convince them about the kingdom of God'. On top of all that, when difficulties arose and opposition resulted he moved to the lecture hall of Tyrannus and 'this went on for two years, so that all the people who lived in the province of Asia, both Jews and Gentiles, heard the word of the Lord' (Acts 19:8-10). Some manuscripts add in reference to this passage 'from 11.00 am until 4.00 pm'. It is hardly surprising that 'God was performing unusual miracles through Paul'. When the Spirit and the word come together, then miracles inevitably occur. The incisiveness of this ministry was far-reaching and a great bonfire of expensive books on the occult resulted. The frontiers of the kingdom of darkness were pushed back and 'in this powerful way the word of the Lord kept spreading and growing stronger' (Acts 19:20).

How important it is to ensure that this priority continues to be maintained within the church. If any church does not have this gift within it, it needs to recognize this with humility and take steps to release the results of this ministry into its life. Books, tapes and videos are all readily available these days, even if there is a shortage of teachers. Leadership within the local church needs to affirm this priority and take practical steps to ensure its place. It is possible to take a traditional view of this fundamental ministry and maintain it in a traditional way without it being effective. This needs to be remedied.

There are two chief sources from which we derive our knowledge of theological matters. These are *natural theology,* which may be described as that knowledge which is derived from material *outside* the Christian revelation, and there is *the Christian revelation,* which, so far as a present-day Christian is concerned, is found recorded authoritatively *inside* the covers of the Bible and *practically* through the prophetic word, but which was, and is, found pre-eminently in the person of our Lord himself. It must always be our first aim to keep our Lord central in all our considerations. The Greek word most nearly equivalent to our word 'inspiration' *theopneustos* or 'God-breathed') occurs only once in the Bible (2 Tim 3:16). The term may be defined as the divine 'in-breathing' into a man by God's Spirit, with the result that he speaks, or writes, with a quality, insight, accuracy and authority which is possible in no other form of speaking or writing.

The following important issues should be borne in mind when attempting to describe this term:

1. Its exact nature, mode and limitations are not accurately defined in Scripture itself.

2. Exactly the same difficulties will be met as in attempting accurately to express the fusion of the human and divine in the person of Jesus Christ. The two problems are almost identical in their form.

3. In studying this problem of inspiration the human mind, believing itself capable of analysing a divine mystery, has again and again demonstrated its presumptive littleness. The student will be well advised, while using all the aids and correctives which scholarship can bring to the subject, to maintain an attitude of reverent caution and not allow himself to be persuaded into destructive criticism which archaeology has consistently and with unfailing persistence disproved.

4. The implications of inspiration were not questioned until recent years. Until the close of the nineteenth century on no subject had the church been more united.

Not only was the word of God used *inside* the early church to instruct, inspire, encourage, correct and guide, but it was used just as powerfully under the ministry of the Holy Spirit *outside* the church in evangelism. The highly organized, carefully planned, strategically-operated evangelism of today is difficult to detect in these early days of the church. It seems rather that they operated on overspill evangelism rather than organized evangelism—wherever the Spirit of God led them and God gave them an opening and an opportunity, they preached and taught the word of God. Most frequently this was in the Temple or the synagogue—but frequently too in the home. In the former they had an audience who at least professed to believe in God and who knew something of the Scriptures, while in the latter there was a much more informal and relaxed atmosphere where people would feel themselves much more comfortable and much less defensive. So it is today—the preaching and teaching of the word of God for evangelism needs to continue in the more formal and often structured services of the church, since all too often the church is a 'pool to fish in' rather than a 'ship to fish from', and the home provides a less threatening environment for sharing truth about Christ. More and more we are finding that homes connected with our church are being used as a 'first base' for evangelism, where people feel they are not souls to be saved, but people to be loved and cared for.

These early Christians, however, were not content to domesticate the word of God. It was not only for the 'in-group', but for all, and they took every possible opportunity to proclaim it—no matter the personal risk involved. It might be before the powerful, controlling body of the Jewish Sanhedrin or on the steps of the famous Areopagus in Athens. It might be in the court of the Roman pro-consul Sergius Paulus or during the tribunals of Felix, Governor of Judea, and of Festus—even when King Agrippa and Bernice were present. Sometimes it was in transit on a chariot belonging to the Ethiopian Chancellor of the Exchequer or in the never-changing environment of a prison. Sometimes it was in the stuffy public lecture hall of Tyrannus, vacated by everybody else because of the unbearable heat of the mid-day sun, and sometimes it was in the open-air in the market-place of Athens. Sometimes it was with individuals in private interview, while at other times it was in the cities and villages. At all times the content of what they had to say was biblical and the wisdom and enabling to say it came from the Holy Spirit.

As constantly they proclaimed God's word *outside* the church, the theme was *Jesus.* In that first bold proclamation of the gospel after the event of Pentecost Peter is concerned to emphasize four things about Jesus. First of all he drew attention to and underlined the fact that Jesus was neither fiction nor fantasy. He was a fact that lived among them and was observable by them. He was 'Jesus of Nazareth'. Who he was was authenticated by what he did. There was visible evidence of invisible reality. Jesus was flesh and what he did was verifiable because 'it happened here among you' (Acts 2:22).

The second thing Peter declared was that Jesus not only lived, but he died. That occurred not just as a result of the viciousness of men, but as a consequence of the sovereignty of God. What appeared to be a senseless, spiteful murder was in fact the outworking and provision and purposes of God (Acts 2:23).

The third strand in Peter's powerful presentation of the gospel was that 'death could not hold its prey'—Jesus defeated death. Four verses from the Psalms (Ps 16:8-11) show that what happened in the resurrection was a direct result of the hand of God. Jesus was the one prophetically promised and divinely released from death (Acts 2:24, 32).

The final declaration about Christ was that he ascended (Acts 2:33-35). We have already observed that between the gospel of Luke and the Acts of the Apostles Jesus 'changed bodies'. In his divine resurrected body he had gone to be with his Father to reign in authority, to intercede on our behalf, and to prepare a place for us. God needed a new body on earth to declare his word and to demonstrate his power—and so the church was born. Such a ministry made deep inroads into human hearts, and caused an earnest response: 'What shall we do, brothers?' (Acts 2:37).

Peter's reply was straightforward enough: 'Turn away from your sins'—repent! Come to a knowledge and understanding of sin in your head—know what sin is and call it that; feel as God feels about sin in your heart; confess that sin with your mouth—for the only way that sin leaves the body is through the mouth; turn from that sin by an act of your will; and where possible make restitution for it. This is repentance. John the Baptist and Jesus had begun there, and this must be the starting place for every life that is determined to confront reality and be revolutionized by the power of God.

'Be baptized in the name of Jesus Christ'—in other words, 'Attend your own funeral service!' Baptism is the symbol of burial, and burial is only for those who are already dead. How often people who have not really been dead to sin have themselves been baptized, and the church has reaped an obvious and treacherous harvest as a result. A faulty teaching and a partial experience of repentance has led to an inadequate practice of baptism and resulted in all the problems that the self-life can bring both individually and corporately. Baptism is to be 'in the name of Jesus'—as if Jesus himself were the baptizer. The hands and lips that are used by the baptizer are simply a substitute for the hands and lips of Christ. No amount of instruction in baptismal classes will be relevant if these crucial elements are omitted.

'So that your sins will be forgiven; and you will receive God's gift, the Holy Spirit.' Our response is equally straightforward—we are to repent; then physically to be identified in baptism with Christ in his death and resurrection; and consequently we are to receive not just one blessing, but two—pardon for the past and provision for the future. The latter is dangerous without the former, and the former is defective without the latter. God does not want us to change from hell-deserving sinners into helpless saints. He so wants to drench us in the Holy Spirit that we will become relevant and effective members of the body of Christ on earth.

Christian initiation has been the subject of a great deal of controversy and confusion—but at the birth of the church it is simple and straightforward enough. Tradition, prejudice and denominational loyalty have created a climate of discussion and debate which has often resulted in divisiveness and disharmony, and ordinary people have frequently been victims of spiritual death as a consequence. It was not so at the beginning! There was a vibrancy and joy, enthusiasm and reality which took the church and its gospel from the religious capital of the world—Jerusalem—to the political capital of the world—Rome—in one generation. The odds against this happening were great, but the life, power and reality that was released was even greater. It is estimated that there were four million Jews in Israel at the time of Pentecost, and so as the Holy Spirit came upon the 120 in that great event there was a statistical ratio of one believer to over thirty-three thousand unbelievers.

The same emphasis on Jesus occurs again and again in Acts—in Acts 3:11-26 Peter speaks simply and clearly about his passion (3:11-14) and his power (Acts 3:15-16)—particularly the power of his name. Significantly, when the church began preaching, they did not preach religion or Christianity. They did not preach a philosophy or a system of ethics or a code of morality. They did not speak as often as we might expect about preaching the gospel—but they did speak about preaching Christ. Peter cried to the confused and convicted multitude on the day of Pentecost, 'Whoever calls on the name of the Lord will be saved' (Acts 2:21). Philip the evangelist, directed by an angel and instructed by the Holy Spirit, intruded into the Bible reading of the Chancellor of Ethiopia as he was travelling in his chariot, and told him 'the good news about Jesus'. An old and unknown disciple of Jesus, Ananias, was persuaded against his will to go and help the feared and suspect Saul of Tarsus with these astonishing instructions from the Lord: 'I have chosen him to serve me, and make my name known to the Gentiles and kings and to the people of Israel' (Acts 9:15). John, in his gospel, sums it up for us with unambiguous clarity: 'As many as received him, to them he gave power to become the sons of God, even to them that believe on his name' (Jn 1:12).

In other words the distinctive content of the earliest Christian teaching can be summed up in one word—*Christ*! It has always been so where reality and effectiveness have accompanied religion. One of the old church fathers declared, 'Were the highest heavens my pulpit, and the whole host of the redeemed my audience, Jesus alone would be my text.' Martin Luther, too, who set the whole of Europe aflame and reverberating with spiritual revolution exclaimed, 'We preach always Christ, and Christ alone, true God and true man. That may seem a monotonous and limited subject, likely to be soon exhausted, but we are never at the end of it.'

'I have tried to preach Jesus Christ, the Jesus Christ not of the gospels only, but the Christ of the gospels and the epistles,' was the simple witness of Alexander Maclaren as he looked back over the creative and impressive years of his ministry in Manchester.

From my Scottish non-liturgical background I was deeply impressed in my first encounters with the Anglican Church in a whole variety of ways—and not least when after a section from the Old Testament or New had been read, there was the simple, categorical statement made—'This is the word of God.' But even more impressive to me was the fact that when the gospels were read in a public service the congregation rose and the reading was concluded with the simple, but for me, moving statement: 'This is the gospel of Christ.' It seemed to me then as it does now that in that context discussion and debate were out of place—and the word read was to be received.

I am grateful to God that as the Spirit moves in the church in these days there is a new hunger for his word. I discover this again and again throughout the United Kingdom. My heart cries out to all my brothers and sisters in Christ to affirm again the necessity and centrality of the word of God. Proclaim it so that people will hear it; teach it so that people will understand it; unfold it so that people will obey it; and inevitably, out of that experience people can do no other than share it.

Although the written word of God is fundamental to all that is recorded in Acts—for God is our ultimate authority, but the Bible is our final court of appeal as to what God said—yet there is another expression of the word of God. This is the prophetic word or the spoken word. We need, of course, to get this in perspective since

> Loyalty to Christ, our risen Saviour, and enthroned Lord, calls for total submission to Scripture, and anyone or any church declining to believe and do what is written there, or failing in practice to be faithful to it is to that extent a rebel against Christ.

So says Dr Jim Packer in his book, *Under God's Word.*[11] That I wholeheartedly endorse, since this is the God-given objective test for our belief and our behaviour. In other words, what the Scripture says, God says. Writing so movingly to his son in the faith, Timothy, as he gets involved in Christian leadership, Paul says: 'All Scripture is inspired by God and is useful for teaching the truth, rebuking error, correcting faults, and giving instruction for right living, so that the person who serves God may be fully qualified and equipped to do every kind of good deed' (2 Tim 3:16-17).

And yet there was and is another way in which God continues to speak to his people. Christianity is essentially a revealed religion. It is God taking the initiative and revealing himself to man in a personal way which calls for a response. Alongside the living Word—the Word of God who became a human being and dwelt among us—and the written word, there is the spoken word. God speaks clearly when the Scriptures are explained and expounded, but also when the prophetic word is expressed. God did not stop speaking to us when the canon of Scripture was completed—although we are not to expect that any further revelation of doctrine will emerge, and unless the spoken word is in accordance with both the living Word and the written word it is not authentic.

Clearly the office or ministry of the prophet was recognized and affirmed in the Acts of the Apostles. Not only is the prophetic ministry of the Old Testament taken seriously on twenty-seven occasions, but the present ministry remains alongside that of the teacher (Acts 13:1). They clearly had a significant leadership function to fulfil which gave direction and stability to the ongoing life of the young church. It is not possible to maintain biblical integrity and simply ignore the existence of this aspect of ministry and leadership (see Acts 11:27; 15:32; 21:10). The prophets were not on the periphery of church life, exercising a suspect ministry, but at its heart fulfilling a vital ministry. There was inevitably the expression of false prophecy (Acts 13:6), but the counterfeit only substantiates the authentic. The bogus is nonsense unless there is also the real.

The fact that it is an unfamiliar ministry today is no ground for rejecting it. Indeed, unless and until the contemporary church discovers the same vibrancy and effectiveness that the young church had we need to be concerned that we do not miss any ingredient of apostolic means if we really desire to achieve and emulate apostolic ends. Within our society today, when someone indicates that he is going to be a minister or pastor or priest or vicar there is still a measure of understanding, approval and acceptance. When someone indicates that he is going to be an evangelist there is immediately an air of mystery introduced, alleviated only by the faint understanding that he is planning to become a mini Billy Graham. But if someone were bold enough to declare that God's calling on his life was to be a prophet, little if any understanding would result—either inside or outside the church. This governs our approach to the prophetic ministry very deeply. As children of our age we start off with a negative approach. Only the revelation of Scripture will help us to deal with this.

The foundational gift of prophecy was given once for all through the apostles for the completion of the New Testament canon of Scripture, but the New Testament clearly experienced different levels of prophecy. In 1 Corinthians 14 there is a contrast made between the gift of tongues and the gift of prophecy (both valid gifts of the Holy Spirit). In Acts there is an inherent contrast between prophecy and teaching (both valid gifts of the risen Christ). The ministry of teaching is the clear declaration of God's word for all time, for all people, and for every situation—a general, comprehensive revelation from the Scriptures. The ministry of prophecy, however, is God's word for this time, and for this specific people, and for this place and in these specific circumstances.

The prophetic ministry gives a 'God framework' for all that the church is and says. If ever this was necessary it is today. The majority of those who live in the United Kingdom do not intelligently know what is meant by 'God' any longer—confusion, bewilderment and scepticism have taken over in this area. Our society has become godless. This is different from immorality—immorality is the result of godlessness, but is distinct from it. The prophet's task is to restore an awareness and an understanding of God. The evangelist, in the exercising of his ministry, emphasizes the reality and relevance of God the Son. The pastor, in the fulfilling of his ministry, dwells on the presence and effectiveness of God the Spirit. The prophet, however, dwells on the existence and significance of God 'the Father the Almighty, maker of heaven and earth, of all that is, seen and unseen'. The gospel is relatively meaningless and irrelevant unless there is this God framework. That is why the Old Testament comes before the New Testament.

In the Old Testament the prophetic ministry is powerful and obtrusive. That is why John the Baptist came before his cousin Jesus Christ of Nazareth: the prophetic ministry prepares the way for the evangelistic ministry. Perhaps one of the main reasons for the poverty of the evangelism which is exercised in the United Kingdom generally is the almost complete absence of the prophetic ministry within and from the contemporary church. Without a God framework Jesus becomes a guru among an increasing number of other gurus within our society! He evokes interest and comment when presented in the media—but little more. Without a God framework the church becomes an institution, a religious club, a social centre—well-meaning and hard-working no doubt, but innocuously adrift from the dimension of the supernatural and the God-like.

If the church's future is going to be effectively different from the past then there needs to be the revival of the prophetic ministry. This is part of the heart-cry of the Bible to God's people today. This ministry is clearly listed among other ministries in the church. To maintain our integrity we need not only to recognize it, but to seek to implement it in the life of the church. The prophet is someone who understands the thoughts of God's mind; feels the emotions of God's heart; sees the intentions and purposes of God's will; and then passes all of this on, no matter what the cost. The prophet is a servant of the Lord whose ministry is utterly simple—he is a voice for God. This vocation implies two things—first of all that God has found two ears that will really listen to him, for the prophetic ministry is essentially a listening ministry; and secondly the prophet is willing to speak for God, since God has found two lips which will speak for him. There are no other practical qualifications required.

He or she (because the prophetic ministry is open to both men and women—another thing which distinguishes it from preaching and teaching in the Bible) does not make herself/himself a prophet. He may be an eighty-year-old Moses or a seventeen-year-old Jeremiah, but he is for ever consciously aware that God has called him for this ministry. He is aware that God has not only called him, but enables him by his Spirit to fulfil his godly ministry. Otherwise false prophecy will result, finding its source often from the flesh and sometimes from the devil. He is for ever conscious that what he has heard or seen is from God—and he will verbalize this or visualize it in a simple and direct way. He is involved first of all in declaring God's message rather than demonstrating God's miracles—miracles do not appear generally to be part of the prophetic ministry, although there are notable exceptions.

From the beginning one of the aspects of the leadership of God's people was the prophetic ministry (Num 11:25-29). Even in the beginning there was hesitancy and controversy when two of the seventy leaders, Eldad and Medad, 'stayed in the camp, and had not gone out to the Tent. There in the camp the Spirit came on them, and they too began to shout like prophets'. Even young Joshua spoke up in alarm and asked Moses to stop them. To this Moses replied: 'Are you concerned about my interests? I wish that the Lord would give his Spirit to all his people and make all of them shout like prophets!'

Jesus, of course, exercised the greatest prophetic ministry. It was clearly recognized on many occasions —for example as he was involved in the resurrection of the dead man at Nain; as he enabled the disciples to feed the 5,000; as he gave sight to the man blind from birth; as he encountered the woman of Samaria at the well; as he became involved with the two disciples on the road to Emmaus. Jesus surely wants to repeat and continue this ministry through his body on earth, the church. Surely he said: 'As the Father sent me, so I send you.' The Dogmatic Constitution on the Church prepared for Vatican II clearly stresses this:

> Christ the Great Prophet who proclaimed the Kingdom of His Father by the testimony of His life and the power of His words continually fulfils His prophetic office until the full glory is revealed. He does this not only through the ministry who teach in His Name and with His authority, but also through the laity.

This is the only ministry which is mentioned in all three passages where the lists of the ministries of the church in the New Testament are mentioned—Romans 12, 1 Corinthians 12 and Ephesians 4. Unhappily it is the ministry that is least talked about, infrequently preached and seldom practised—and then only with great hesitancy in the Western church. It takes more faith to prophesy than to preach. It requires the faith that believes God still speaks today and he wants mouths through which he can communicate. Our trouble often is that we are better at talking than listening—and prophecy, as we have already noted, is essentially a listening ministry. It also requires a faith which believes that God could use people in this way, for this was one of the central reasons why Pentecost happened—not so that we would sing charismatic choruses, but so that God could speak to the world. When God sends renewal it is for the sake of the world, not for the sake of the church. God often has more negative feelings about his church than about his world. He is looking for ears that will hear and voices that will speak for him to his world.

We need then to overcome the often-felt, if not often-stated, objections to this crucial ministry. It is often criticized that it appears to string Scripture phrases together. This must surely be a weak criticism, since the prophetic word and the written word come from the same source. The Revelation of St John at the end of the Bible is more than half Scripture phrases.

Others have felt that prophetic words they have heard are often simple and appear to be trivial. There is the constant danger in our traumatic world that we are constantly looking for the sensational rather than the spiritual. In 520 BC Haggai gave this remarkable prophetic word to the people of God: 'I will be with you—that is my promise (1:13). That was all he said, and not another word came to God's people for a month. It may well seem to be the most unsensational of the utterances of the servants of the Lord, and yet what could be more dynamic or dramatic if we were really prepared to grasp its implications.

Most common of all the objections to the prophetic ministry, however, is that it is dangerous. Of course, this must be faced—it is! It can effectively give guidance for future needs. Luke recalls in Acts 11:27-28 how the 'prophets went from Jerusalem to Antioch'. Having arrived there, 'One of them, named Agabus, stood up and by the power of the Holy Spirit predicted that a severe famine was about to come over all the earth [when Claudius was Emperor].' This is either right or wrong. This will either be authenticated visibly and unmistakably or dismissed as emotional hysteria. However, it happened. Historians record the situation and explain that the Roman farmers had for years been taking from the land without putting anything back. The well-fed empire had been taking so much from Mother Nature that she rebelled against man's greed.

Nobody knew, however, the effect of this except a little group of Christians in Antioch. God gives these warnings not so that we will avoid difficulties like this, but so that we will prepare for them. The early church received this prophetic word and Barnabas and Paul became joint-treasurers of the famine relief fund before they became great missionaries. One of the marks of authentic prophecy which is clearly demonstrated here was—it happens!

Prophecy, as well as giving guidance for future needs, can often give direction for the church's ministry. The enthralling chapter in early church history (Acts 12:25-16:5) when the church began to move out in 'overseas mission' into Asia Minor was initiated by the prophetic ministry. Specific directions were given about manpower and resources: 'While they were serving the Lord and fasting, the Holy Spirit said to them, "Set apart for me Barnabas and Saul, to do the work to which I have called them." They fasted and prayed, placed their hands on them and sent them off' (Acts 13:2-4). Notice that in the church at Antioch as well as teachers in the leadership there were prophets (Acts 13:1).

The prophetic word has a profound effect upon the lives of Christians in the local church fellowship, for the prophet 'speaks to people and gives them help, encouragement and comfort' (1 Cor 14:3). It can readily be seen how dangerous this ministry is if practised irresponsibly and allowed without proper control. Human lives are affected, not just human ideas. However, the way to handle the abuse of something is seldom to eliminate its use, but rather to make sure that it is used properly.

Testing prophecies

There are certain clear tests to be applied in order that a prophetic word is authenticated. Let me give a check-list to allay fears that the flesh will have its way—or even more disastrous, the devil. The result of that will surely be confusion and the dishonouring of the name of the Son of God.

Does the prophetic word give honour to the Son of God? (Jn 16:14; 1 Cor 12:1-4)

The primary work of the Holy Spirit is to glorify the Son. If he is truly the source of the prophetic word then its content will honour and glorify him, although his name may not be mentioned overtly. The prophetic word will never contradict the Son of God.

Does the prophetic word strengthen the church? (1 Cor 14)

In 1 Corinthians 14 the word 'help' *(oikodomē,* from two Greek words denoting the act of building—*oikos,* 'a home' and *demō,* 'to build') occurs seven times. *Oikodomē* is used only figuratively in the New Testament in the sense of the promotion of spiritual growth. The prophetic word exists to do just that. It is not there to crush or to condemn—although sometimes weakness has to be dealt with in order that strength can result. The effect of the prophetic word is to strengthen and not weaken.

Does the prophetic word agree with the Scriptures?

Any prophetic word which is clearly contrary to the Scriptures is automatically to be regarded as wrong. God never contradicts his Son nor does he ever act contrary to his word.

Does the prophetic word come with sensitivity? (1 Cor 13:13)

Even in correction and rebuke love is always the hallmark of the Holy Spirit's presence. There can always be understanding if not agreement—although understanding is never to be mistaken for agreement, nor is tenderness ever to be mistaken for softness and compromise.

Does the prophetic word come from someone who is sincere? (Mt 7:15-20)

Jesus quite clearly indicates that false prophets can always be distinguished by the visible fruit of their lives. The true prophet will be authenticated not only by what he says, but also by what he does. By implication Jesus would not give such a clear warning against the false unless the true had an important role to fulfil.

It is because of this particular test that we have become very reserved, cautious and hesitant about allowing the visitor, who has come into our church and whom we do not know, to bring a prophetic word to us.

Does the prophetic word come from someone who is in submission to the local church leadership? (Acts 20:28-31)

Paul gives this heart-felt warning to the Ephesian elders, for strong personalities with independent spirits caused splits, divisions and confusion in the New Testament church (e.g. 1 Cor 1). It is no different today. It is strange how Christians will willingly submit to civic and political authority as a clear matter of Christian principle even though they may be at variance with the stance they are taking, and yet are unwilling to submit to church authority when they are at variance there. It is a strange inconsistency which often passes as acceptable and justifiable. There are those whose prophetic utterance needs to be cancelled out on the basis of this alone.

Does the prophetic word come from someone willing to have that word weighed and scrutinized? (1 Cor 14:29)

Sometimes the way that a prophetic word is given gives no room for scrutiny and weighing. It comes in a form which is authoritative and is already invested in its wording with an affirmation of divine approval. This creates a serious problem.

The task of the one who is giving the prophetic word is to give it—the responsibility of the church leadership is to ensure that it is the word of the Lord. This 'weighing of the word' is the rule, not the exception. Anyone giving such a prophetic word must be open to this and resist feeling upset, threatened or put down by it.

Does the prophetic word come from someone who is stable? (1 Cor 12:2, 14:32)

A speaker may be 'taken over' by an evil spirit, but never by the Holy Spirit. The gift of prophecy—like all the other gifts of God—is entirely within the control of the one to whom it has been given. The accompaniment of uncontrolled sobbing and histrionics puts a question mark over the validity of what is being communicated.

Does the prophetic word have its own self-evidence? (Deut 18:22)

A great deal of prophecy is *forth*-telling rather than *fore*-telling. It is a direct word from God in a specific set of circumstances and usually confirms by encouragement and exhortation. Only on rare occasions will prophecy predict some future event—and when that is so then the test of its authenticity lies in the prophecy itself. Its reality will be demonstrated by the fulfilment or the lack of it.

Does the prophetic word come from someone who is peaceful? (Gal 5:22)

I am not referring here to someone who is lethargic or complacent or off-hand. The Holy Spirit is the Spirit of balance, and agitation and anxiety and tenseness are not evidence of his presence or his life.

Having defined and described the supernatural love of Christ on the cross made available to us by the Holy Spirit, Paul goes on to say to the Corinthian church in that climate (1 Cor 14:1-4):

> It is love, then, that you should strive for. Set your heart on spiritual gifts, especially the gift of proclaiming God's message [*propheteuete*]. The one who speaks in strange tongues does not speak to others, but to God, because no one understands him. He is speaking secret truths by the power of the Spirit. But the one who proclaims God's message speaks to people and gives them help, encouragement, and comfort. The one who speaks in strange tongues helps only himself, but the one who proclaims God's message helps the whole church (GNB, adapted).

God is not an idol, deaf, dumb and helpless. He is our heavenly Father whose love is backed by his power and whose power is tempered by his love—and he wants to be on speaking terms with his family. We need to develop the facility to hear what he is saying in order to do what he wants.

7

Share It—or Lose It!

One of the great Christian leaders of this century, Dr John R. Mott concluded: 'If a man has a religion, he must either give it up or give it away. If it is not true, he must give it up; if it is true, he must give it away.' So far as Acts is concerned the good news of Jesus Christ did not spread in such a rapid and romantic way because of a missionary society or because of an attractive programme constructed by an enthusiastic committee and supported by a plethora of gifted individuals. The way that the gospel of our Lord Jesus spread was not as a result of a deliberate decision at all, but simply the natural overflow of ordinary men and women whose lives had been filled with the Holy Spirit. Dr James Kennedy of Evangelism Explosion fame observes:

> If you were an outstanding and gifted evangelist with an international reputation and under God you could win one thousand persons for Christ every night of every year—how long would it take you to win the whole world for Christ? Ignoring the population explosion, over ten thousand years. But if you are a true disciple for Christ, and if you are able to win, under God, just one person for Christ each year—and you trained that one person to win one

other person to Christ each year, how long would it take to win the whole world to Christ? Answer, just thirty-two years!

Originally it was for this reason that the Holy Spirit came—to enable us to be effective and relevant in sharing our faith. There is something natural about wanting to keep what we have come to possess. It often takes a miracle—the supernatural ministry of God—to release us from our possessiveness. The summary of the Acts of the Apostles is in the six little words of Acts 6:3: 'I give you what I have.' This is not only a summary of Acts, but a summary or a complete prescription for spiritual health.

All over this land within the church many are fearful, hesitant and unwilling to receive what God wants to give. We live below—often very far below—the fullness of our inheritance in Christ. A great deal of our spiritual poverty and ineptitude can be explained simply in that we are not because we have not, and we have not because we receive not. Tradition, prejudice and fear all play their part in our culpable contentment with less than all that God wants to give. But the other end of this situation is equally common and sad—that we want to keep what we have. We justify this selfishness in all sorts of plausible and convincing ways.

It is worth remembering, however, that 400–500 people die of starvation every hour, and a further 6,000 will die of other causes. At the same time more than 14,000 new babies will be born in that short space of time. This means that, at the present rate of explosion, the world population *increases* by approximately 8,000 every hour or 200,000 every day, the majority of whom will be born into areas where there is little or no knowledge of Christ. Although there are 1,000 million professing Christians in the world, this leaves well over

2,000 million who are not. To emphasize the magnitude of the task confronting the church, there are twice as many non-Christians in the world today as at the turn of the century. Moreover, by the turn of the next century the world population will have doubled. Some of those destined to live—and ultimately to die—without Christ are within our own land. Some are within our own street and even within our own homes. It is much easier to argue and discuss with our fellow Christians which English translation of the Bible is best or whether speaking in tongues is the initial evidence of the baptism in the Holy Spirit, or if tithing is only an Old Testament principle and not for New Testament Christians, or whether the church hall should be painted green or blue, or whether we should have chairs rather than pews in the church, than to share the good news of Christ with a world that is dying spiritually on its feet.

The church is the only society on earth which exists primarily for its non-members. How uncomfortable! It is much easier to be absorbed with the 1.5% in Britain who know Christ than with the 98.5% who do not. It is much more comfortable to spend our time, energy and gift on committees rather than on conversions. It is much less threatening to be concerned about and committed to traditional (and often denominational) structures than to be exposed to, and to experience, life in the Spirit. It is all too familiar for the church to be caught up with people *inside* rather than people *outside* the church. Acts lays a sharp axe at the root of this particular comfortable selfishness. To read it and to understand it is to be aware of the heartbreak of God for the lost and to realize the peril of disregard for the fundamental reason for the out-pouring of the Holy Spirit—to make us witnesses.

A witness is a man who says, 'I know this is true.' In a court of law a witness is unable to give a carried story in evidence; it must be his own personal experience. There was a time when that great Puritan, John Bunyan, was not sure. What worried him was that the Jews think their religion the best religion; the Mohammedans think their religion the best religion. What if Christianity were to be a *think*-so religion too? A witness does not say, 'I think so,' he says, 'I know.' But the Holy Spirit has come to communicate certainty and security to the human mind and heart, and then wisdom, sensitivity and boldness to the human voice.

In the second place a real witness is not the witness of words, but of deeds. In Acts 4:13-17 the Jerusalem Council (largely comprising most of the seventy-one who judged and condemned Jesus a few weeks earlier) were impressed by the changed lives not only of the man who had been delivered, but also of the disciples. When H.M. Stanley had discovered David Livingstone in Central Africa, and when he had spent some time with him, he said, 'If I had been with him any longer I would have been compelled to be a Christian, and he never spoke to me about it at all.' The sheer weight of the witness of this man's life was irresistible. Confronted with the visible reality of changed lives, the Jerusalem Council of the Jewish leaders, elders and the teachers of the Law could only conclude, 'We cannot deny it' (Acts 4:16)—however hard it is to swallow. This giving of visible evidence of the invisible reality which we have experienced and declare is an inescapable part of being a witness. Edgar Wallace, the author of many thriller novels, had a many-coloured character and lived a very mixed life. Up the road from him lived a Methodist minister, Benjamin Hillier. Wallace concluded, in spite of his inability to be more rational about it, 'I can never be an atheist while I live near Benjamin Hillier.' The Holy Spirit has come to credit us with the risen life of Christ and to enable us to live the Jesus life in his power.

Thirdly, it is one of the most suggestive facts that in the Greek language the word for '*witness*' and the word for '*martyr*' is the same word—*martus*. A witness had to be ready to become a martyr. In other words, to be a witness means to be loyal, no matter what the cost. Brother Andrew was once sitting with another Christian on a bus in Vietnam. They saw a man carrying a basket walking in front of the bus. It was during a time of intense fighting and constant guerrilla attacks in that lacerated country. 'Watch out!' said the Christian. 'In that basket there might well be a bomb!'

'Why are you so afraid?' asked Brother Andrew.

'That man may be a Vietcong who will throw himself and the basket at the bus,' came the reply. 'He doesn't mind if he dies, but I do!'

Brother Andrew commented on this incident, 'That sums up the ineffectiveness of so much of the Church today!'

How many Christians are willing to lay down their lives for Jesus Christ? For fear that we put this in the category of the extravagant and the unlikely, it is a simple record of fact that in this century alone there have probably been more Christian martyrs than in the entire history of the Christian church put together. Hundreds of thousands have died for their faith in the Congo (now Zaire), Kenya, Burundi, Papua, Ecuador, China, Russia, Rumania, and many other countries.

Great and right publicity has been given to the horrifying story of famine in Ethiopia. The Live Aid music extravaganza simultaneously sponsored in Wembley Stadium and in the USA, described as the greatest show of all time, captured the heart, imagination and admiration of millions throughout the world in its attempt to draw attention to and gather funds for the starving Ethiopians. However, towards the end of

1984, when some of the horror of famine in Ethiopia was beginning to dawn on many of us, 748 churches were closed in the Ethiopian province of Sidamo. Almost involuntarily, the thought arises: 'But that, surely, is not as terrible as the millions of people who are dying of hunger?'

'No, indeed,' writes Brother Andrew,

> But things have gone so far that we have to weigh one evil against the other. It also means that we weigh one good deed against another: food aid against help for persecuted Christians. If only we understood that it's all linked together. Famine and persecution against the church go hand in hand . . . and it costs millions of lives . . . since the Marxist revolution in 1975, the Ethiopian refugees have been telling us about the mismanagement by the government in Addis Ababa. But no one listened. The thing that angers me most, though, is the fact that my fellow Christians have now been persecuted for ten years. As I write to you, at least a thousand church leaders and ministers are in prison. Further, while millions of pounds have been given for food aid, 45,000 Bibles have been stored in a customs warehouse for several years, waiting for clearance by the Ethiopian authorities.[12]

While many of us were recovering from overeating here in the West during our Christmas celebrations of 1984 and complaining that the quality and variety of TV programmes over Christmas had plummeted remarkably, Kostadin Kalmukov, a Christian from the east Bulgarian town of Karnobat, presently serving a sentence of five years in the prison of Stara Zagora, was beaten unconscious by prison warders because he refused to work on Christmas Day. He was then thrown naked into a punishment cell. Because Kostadin was in danger of dying from the cold, he was taken out of the cell three days later.

This is all pretty powerful and dramatic, and against this background our own willingness and attempts at witnessing seem pretty feeble. However, the same Holy Spirit, who has enabled and continues to enable ordinary Christian men and women to be loyal no matter what the cost, wants to come upon us for the same purpose. It is fruitless and destructive simply to remain feeling guilty over our unwillingness and ineptitude at witnessing. It is fulfilling and satisfying to allow the Holy Spirit to enable us to become what he has always wanted us to be—witnesses!

When a man writes a book he does so for some reason—and often for more than one reason. A number of reasons have been adduced as to why Luke wrote the Acts of the Apostles. For example, he was quite clearly commending Christianity to the Roman government. Again and again he goes out of his way to show how courteous Roman magistrates were to Paul (see Acts 13:12; 16:35ff; 18:12; 19:31; 23:29; 25:25). This was at a time when Christians were disliked and persecuted. Again, one of Luke's aims was to show that Christianity was a universal religion for all men of every country. This was one of the things which the Jews found hard to grasp. They had a firm idea that they were God's chosen people and they were convinced that God did not have any use for any other nation. So in Acts we see Philip preaching to the Samaritans; Stephen, in the longest sermon in the New Testament, making Christianity a universal thing and being killed for it; Peter accepting Cornelius into the church; the Christians preaching to the Gentiles at Antioch; Paul travelling far and wide winning men of all kinds to faith in and allegiance to Christ. Perhaps the peak of all this, and a great historical watershed, is the great decision by the church to accept the Gentiles on equal terms with the Jews with no reservations (Acts 15). Clearly Christianity is presented in Acts as a religion which knows no bounds.

However significant these aims might be, they were secondary to the primary reason that Acts is a record of how ordinary people, filled with the Holy Spirit, were concerned to be obedient to the risen Christ and fulfil his directive, 'When the Holy Spirit comes upon you, you will be filled with power, and you will be witnesses for me in Jerusalem, in all of Judea and Samaria, and to the ends of the earth' (Acts 1:8). A great New Testament scholar has said that the title of Acts might be, *How they brought the Good News from Jerusalem to Rome.* Undoubtedly Luke's great aim was to show the expansion of Christianity, using with faith the means God provided. He sets the facts down with all his clinical expertise how Christianity was born in a tiny, unpromising corner of Palestine and within one generation had reached and was influencing the heart of the Roman Empire—Rome itself.

C. H. Turner points out how Acts falls into six sections, each one ending with a progress report.

1. Acts 1:1-6:7. This section tells of the church at Jerusalem and the preaching of Peter. It ends with the summary: 'And so the word continued to spread. The number of disciples in Jerusalem grew larger and larger, and a great number of priests accepted the faith.'

2. Acts 6:8-9:31. Here is the record of the spread of Christianity through Palestine and the martyrdom of Stephen, followed by the preaching in Samaria. It ends with the summary: 'And so it was that the church throughout Judea, Galilee and Samaria had a time of peace. Through the help of the Holy Spirit it was strengthened and grew in numbers, as it lived in reverence for the Lord.'

3. Acts 9:32-12:24. Paul's dramatic and strategic conversion is included here as well as the extension of the

church to Antioch, and the reception of Cornelius the Gentile into the church by Peter. Its concluding summary is: 'Meanwhile the word of God continued to spread and grow.'

4. Acts 12:25-16:5. Now the church is extending through Asia Minor and the remarkable preaching tour of Galatia is recorded. It ends with a stabilizing confidence: 'So the churches were made stronger in the faith and grew in numbers every day.'

5. Acts 16:6-19:20. The extension of the church continues into Europe and Paul's ministry is being blessed by God in great Gentile cities like Ephesus and Corinth. The summary is intriguing: 'In this powerful way the word of the Lord kept spreading and growing stronger.'

6. Acts 19:21-28:31. This tells of Paul's arrival in Rome and his imprisonment there. It ends with positive personal triumph in the face of difficulty. It shows that the book's task has been completed and Christianity has come from the religious capital of the world—Jerusalem—to the political capital of the world—Rome. 'He preached about the kingdom of God and taught about the Lord Jesus Christ, speaking with all boldness and freedom.'

The late Professor William Barclay of Glasgow University said: 'In reading Acts a confidence is born that no historian ever had better sources and no historian ever used his sources more accurately and more honestly.'

Witnessing, then, is not simply a theological concept in the early church, nor is it an oft-repeated shibboleth, but if worship is the first consequence of the outpouring of the Holy Spirit on the day of Pentecost—and it is (Acts 2:1-13)—witnessing follows immediately afterwards. In *Evangelism in the Early Church* Michael Green concludes that:

> All Christians were convinced that Jesus Christ was God's last word to man, the one who brought as much of God to us as we could appreciate in the only terms we could take it in, the terms of human life; the one who in dying and rising again was manifestly vindicated in His claims and achievements. This they all believed in common: their modes of expressing it depended to a large extent on their own intellectual and spiritual background and on that of their hearers.[13]

This was not the studied rhetoric and flowery eloquence of the professional Greek sophist. These itinerant professional Greeks with their impressive flow of lofty words gave all the appearance of wisdom, but in the sight of God it was all empty, irrelevant foolishness. As we have already noted, the early Christians were not so much declaring Bible words or a gospel formula as they were proclaiming Christ himself. Writing in his journal for the 17th July, 1739, John Wesley simply records:

> I rode to Bradford five miles from Bath. Some persons had pitched on a convenient place, on the top of a hill under which the town lies; there I offered Christ to about 1,000 people, for wisdom, righteousness, sanctification and redemption.[14]

Accuracy and faithfulness in our doctrine is fundamentally important, but initially evangelism consists in offering people Christ.

My very first experience of being gripped by the preaching of Christ, not only mentally and emotionally but physically was while I was still an undergraduate at the University of Glasgow during an Easter vacation. I was struggling with my beliefs and convictions as a result of my domestic circumstances and also because of the profound impact of the academic life on me. I attended an Easter conference organized by the Inter-Varsity Fellowship in a delightful setting on the banks of Loch Lomond. It was there for the first time that I confronted Professor James S. Stewart. His preaching and writing were to become one of the major influences on my life. He himself exemplified to me what he was later to write about in his book, *Teach Yourself Preaching*.

> Ernest Raymond, novelist and essayist, has described the most impressive sermon he ever heard. In itself, he relates, the sermon was ordinary enough: intellectually negligible, aesthetically ragged. Its construction was faulty, its delivery abominable. Yet its effect was overwhelming . . . 'I think he spoke for an hour, and not a man of us moved, and most of us were very quiet all that night . . .' It is one thing to learn the techniques and mechanics of preaching: it is quite another to preach a sermon which will draw back the veil and make the barriers fall that hide the face of God.[15]

James Stewart was the first to 'draw back the veil' so far as I was concerned. Others have done so since to a greater or lesser degree. But this sort of impact was the effect of the witnessing and evangelism in the early church of Acts. This can only be the consequence of the ministry of the Holy Spirit.

These Acts Christians unlocked a precious secret. The thirty years of the church described in Acts is the time of her greatest success in proportion to her numbers. With a bewildering swiftness she grew numerically from eleven men to 120 in chapter 1 to 3,120 in chapter 2. By the beginning of chapter 4 another 5,000 men (presumably this excludes the women and young people who were captivated by Christ) had been added to this. Legitimately we might assume that in excess of 10,000 were now born anew into the kingdom of God—

and the record has hardly got started!

But not only is there dramatic and impressive numerical growth, there is also a profound impact by the church socially. Acts has an eloquent testimony to the fact that it was not only slaves and beggars who responded to the good news of Christ, but also those with highly significant positions in society—governors and at least one Chancellor of the Exchequer.

Geographically two new continents were invaded with the gospel. Europe and Africa joined Asia as a result of the developing life of the church. To ponder this in view of the church's inauspicious beginnings, lack of resources and poverty of good connections in high places is quickly to become aware of the dimension of the miraculous. Clearly we are not up to their standard of mission and evangelism today. The question needs to be asked if we are to maintain our integrity and respond to the calling of God upon our lives: 'What did they have that we do not have?' Perhaps we have struggled with this question in the light of the plain evidence of Acts because basically we are asking the wrong question when we ask that one. Light will only begin to break for us when we ask another question today: 'What did they not have that we do have?'

A number of things now begin to appear which may well be misunderstood and misconstrued—yet remain as incontrovertible evidence. They did not, for example, depend on the size of the weekly collection for encouragement to do what God wanted them to do or go where God wanted them to go. Never once do you find a treasurer who has worked out how much per member is required to keep pace with immediate expenditure, far less developing new work. Their mission—in whatever sphere—never seems to be related to the health or otherwise of some fund set up for the purpose. In fact Peter defines its relevance in two remarkable statements of six words each: 'I have no money at all,' and: 'I give you what I have' (Acts 3:6). This would be an effective summary of the climate of Acts. It would be foolish and irresponsible to ignore and despise money as a factor in any sphere of life, but how often the vision of God has died and the work of God has been frustrated when instead of following the vision and doing the work we have asked questions like, 'How much will it cost?', 'What funds do we have?' and, 'How can we raise the money for it?'

Nor did the early church have buildings and equipment set aside exclusively for 'the work of God'. Again it can be helpful to have facilities whereby we can fulfil our task in a way which impresses the world and takes some of the difficulty and drudgery out of it for us. It is not too far a step, however, to get to the place where we are much too concerned about, and then rely upon, the means and lose sight of the end. Sophistication and smartness can sometimes be substitutes for widespread effectiveness. These early Christians simply used what they had, but it was impregnated by the power and wisdom of God.

Again they seemed to be singularly lacking in some of the superstructure of church life that has come to be accepted and expected in the church today. For example, there was no denominational headquarters which supported and maintained a considerable bureaucratic machine with its well-thought-out administration and departments. In denominational life today new departments with interesting names appear to spring up with ever-increasing momentum. New appointments occur and think-tanks are set up to organize strategy from a distance. Their reports, memos, surveys and analyses are all very impressive and certainly appear to justify the appointment of those who produce them, but what real use are they? Activity has often overtaken relevance and spiritual effectiveness. This way of going about the things of the kingdom of God is absent from the Acts story.

On examination they did not set up Christian institutions within their society—like schools, hospitals and homes for the elderly. Indeed they seemed to be remarkably free from philanthropic institutions. Their concentration seemed to be on their homes. These were the centres of service and activity. It was towards these that people gravitated. It would be negative and untrue to the facts of contemporary Christian living to disallow these facilities in the fulfilling of our calling under God, but it is so dangerously easy for us to build up things which make it easier for us to trust ourselves. The early church was comparatively free from that kind of danger.

The precious secret which Acts unlocks for us is that in their mission and evangelism they lacked the things which made them self-sufficient. The result of this was that they were driven back on God. Lacking human resources, they were drawn back on divine resources. Though they had fewer things than we have, they were so very much richer than we are.

Some years ago I lunched with a missionary who had recently returned to the United Kingdom from the Amazonian jungle, where he had been working in Bible translation for many years. I wondered what his immediate reactions were to the impact of our British culture on him after a long absence. His reply has remained with me over the years. 'In Britain,' he said, 'we have everything and yet we have nothing, but among my Indians they have nothing and yet they have everything.' Knowing him, I'm sure that he was not advocating a return to a primitive lifestyle, but he was making a plea for a greater simplicity in our lifestyle and a refusal to be enamoured with things. Such a plea needs to be made not only socially, but also spiritually. Herein lies a major part of the secret of Acts evangelism!

The strategy which they adopted was often in sharp contrast to the way we set about winning people to Jesus Christ. For example there was a marked confidence and fearlessness in confronting adults rather than children. It is not that children are unimportant or unable to respond to the gospel of Christ, but it is ten times easier to influence and affect a child than it is an adult. A Sunday school or a youth organization is much quicker to fill than a church. I was brought up on the dictum: 'If you get the children, you get the parents.' I suppose not only consciously, but subconsciously I absorbed that and believed it. Maybe there was a time when that was truer than it is today. The facts of the matter today are that even when you get the children you do not always get the children! Six out of seven children who have been in the Sunday schools of Britain will leave between the years of ten and thirteen. This is not to negate the validity of child evangelism (after all, the parable of the sower needs constantly to be kept in mind when we are in danger of discouragement), but I wish to question the conviction and the consequences which flow from it if it is to be the main thrust in confronting our society with the gospel of Jesus Christ. In the Acts strategy in evangelism they undoubtedly went for adults rather than children.

Another contrasting part of their strategy in mission was that they went for men rather than women. This is not taught, but it is an observable fact. Again, there is an underlying feeling today that if you get the wife to respond to Christ the husband will follow. This has seldom been my experience. Much more likely, when you win the wife to Christ you are taking on board a very sensitive family problem. On the other hand, when a man is won to Christ there is a greater likelihood of getting his family. I cannot quote statistics to prove these things, but I have seen them happen.

Compared with the way we go about things today, the Acts Christians never attempted to cheapen the gospel in order to get people to respond to it. Dietrich Bonhoeffer, who paid the ultimate price for his convictions and loyalty to truth and righteousness when he met his death at the hands of the SS Black Guards on the 9th April, 1945, resisted this trend in the contemporary church.

> Cheap grace [Bonhoeffer said] is the deadly enemy of our Church. We are fighting today for costly grace. Cheap grace means grace sold on the market like cheapjacks' wares. The sacraments, the forgiveness of sin, and the consolations of religion are thrown away at cut prices. Grace is represented as the Church's inexhaustible treasury, from which she showers blessings with generous hands, without asking questions or fixing limits. Grace without price; grace without cost! . . . Cheap grace is the preaching of forgiveness without requiring repentance, baptism without church discipline, Communion without confession, absolution without personal confession. Cheap grace is grace without discipleship, grace without the Cross, grace without Jesus Christ, living and incarnate . . .
>
> Costly grace is the treasure hidden in the field; for the sake of it a man will gladly go and sell all that he has. It is the pearl of great price to buy which the merchant will sell all his goods. It is the kingly rule of Christ, for whose sake a man will pluck out the eye which causes him to stumble, it is the call of Jesus Christ at which the disciple leaves his nets and follows him. Costly grace is the gospel which must be sought again and again, the gift which must be asked for, the door at which a man must knock.[16]

In the Acts church they preached a full gospel. They began by calling for repentance from sin. Elsewhere I have outlined the content and implications of repentance, but here I want to affirm its fundamental necessity to reality in our relationship with God. I hear Christian testimonies with a fair degree of regularity and often I am left with a feeling that the gospel that has been preached and received is the gospel of the offers—respond to God and he will bless you, heal you, give you peace, ensure freedom, instil hope, and so on. All that is true, but the initial impact of the gospel is the love of God meeting the sin of man. We have been God-resistant and rebellious over any intrusion and interference by God in our lives. He has caught us and confronted us with weapons in our hands. He has surely dealt with sin, but before he can deal with sin in us our repentance is required.

As they proclaimed Christ they declared him to be both Lord and Christ. To declare him to be Saviour only is to misrepresent him and to propagate faulty spiritual birth. If cheap grace is *the* deadly enemy of the church, then it is the result of receiving salvation without recognizing that the One who saves demands lordship in our lives. Never once does the Bible talk about getting people to accept Jesus as Saviour. When we acknowledge him as Lord, at that point he becomes our Saviour. To become a Christian in essence is putting our lives under the lordship of Christ. For every occasion in the Bible Jesus is spoken of as Saviour, he is spoken of as Lord twenty-nine times. The practical implications of this for living are devastatingly profound and radical. Mental assent to doctrinal statements will not suffice.

The way in which heart-repentance and spiritual understanding of the lordship of Christ was declared was in fact by baptism by immersion in water. To be sure, it is heavily symbolical, but the spiritual implications of being crucified with Christ and being raised to newness of life are not optional, but obligatory. An unbaptized Christian would have been a mysterious anomaly beyond the grasp of the ordinary Acts Christian.

In all of this the baptism in the Holy Spirit was not only meaningful terminology, but meaningful experience. God never intended the sons of his family and the citizens of his kingdom to do his will and fulfil his purposes in their own human strength. If beginning in the Spirit and continuing in the flesh is frequent human experience it was never the intention of God that it should be so. To be relevant, functioning members of the body of Christ on earth we need the gift of the Holy Spirit and the gifts which he wants to give us to fulfil our task and satisfy Christ, the head of the body.

Inevitably the idea of leading someone to Christ and not integrating them really and actually into Christ's body, like an arm or leg to a physical body, would never have occurred to these Acts Christians. To them an unattached Christian would have been an unbelievable phenomenon. They recognized that there was no such thing as isolated religion anywhere in the Bible. To come into a living relationship with God through Christ was to enter into a living relationship with Christians too. And so their gospel comprised repentance before God, recognition of and submission to Jesus Christ as both Lord and Saviour, baptism in water, baptism in the Holy Spirit, and a vital integration by personal commitment into the living body of Christ on earth.

Another vital and very clear characteristic of their evangelism was its supernaturalness. To achieve their objective they knew that in a word-proof society it was necessary to appeal not just to one of the human senses, but to two—sight as well as hearing. Demonstrating the gospel was as important as declaring it. We have so emphasized the cerebral content and appeal of the gospel that we have underestimated its obvious, physical evidence—and that with sad results. They must have been fully aware that it was by the foolishness of preaching that men were saved, and yet they were equally aware that unless things were happening which were beyond human explanation, then men's attention would not be arrested and their minds would not be challenged.

We have noticed how real and profound was their impact on society. We have observed how they were dependent on God in a way that we know little about. We have explored some of the elements in their strategy which strike a vivid contrast to the strategy we adopt today. We now need to see that their effectiveness did not depend on their organizational ability in evangelism nor on the techniques which they adopted. The fundamental reason for their success was that they were involved in overspill evangelism. You can only spill over when you are full up. The fuller you are, the more effort you require to keep what you are filled with in rather than to get it out.

Some time ago I was shopping with my wife in a nearby town. Shopping has never been my favourite occupation, necessary though it is. After long experience I have found that there are certain devices that can help to make it at least bearable. One of these is to visit a tea shop at least once during the expedition. We were doing that on this occasion and enjoying a cup of coffee in an almost empty self-service restaurant when I noticed a little boy walking, bent almost double, towards a table. He looked quite a pitiable sight—slow and moving with great difficulty—until I realized what he was doing. The girl at the counter had filled his glass to overflowing with coca-cola and he was carrying it back to where his parents were sitting. He was too young, I suppose, to know that he would have been better to stop and drink some before he went any further. The result was a very noticeable effort and intense concentration to keep the coke in the glass. When something is full to overflowing it is easier to let it spill over than it is to prevent it doing so.

So it was in Acts. That whole history book is completely impossible to understand if you remove or neglect chapter 2. All that occurred afterwards is related to what happened then. They were involved in overspill evangelism rather than organized evangelism. It is not that the organization of mission is wrong, but it can quickly become a substitute for the reality of what we are supposed to do. If Christians are only half-full, then evangelism can easily become a duty and a drudgery. We very quickly become preoccupied with techniques and tactics. We quickly begin to set up classes and teach-ins and seminars on evangelism. These have their place—but only as a means for channelling the life which is already there!

These early Christians never mistook the necessity for two things, both of which were their inheritance in Christ. One was their spiritual birth and the other was their spiritual baptism. These were first-generation Christians. Something fundamental had to happen to them to bring them into spiritual reality. They had no precedent to follow nor did they have a tradition to copy and accept. It was a personal and dynamic confrontation for each one individually. One of the most destructive things that we have had to reckon with since that time is the 'faith of our fathers'. There is now a form to recognize; a tradition to be absorbed; prejudices to be reckoned with. Some of this is good and has brought stability and security, but much of it has ministered death to Christians individually and corporately. In spiritual terms there are no such beings as second generation Christians, since God has no grandsons. These Acts Christians were free from what has become the hand of death on the contemporary church.

The other aspect of their experience—their spiritual baptism—was equally real to them. As we have seen, their baptism in the Holy Spirit came at the beginning of their mission, not at the end. It was not a reward for growth and spiritual success, but a gift to enable them to function properly and effectively. They spilled over as a result of this filling and so conferences on evangelism and evangelistic committees were not as necessary as we seem to find them. God had manifested his life to them in two of nature's most destructive elements—wind and fire. They knew the reality of the blowing and the burning of God upon their lives. Both must have been unforgettable experiences, but the effect is contained in twenty-eight chapters.

Fundamentally the message of Acts is that only the things which God does by his Spirit will last for eternity. As a book it stands as a warning from God to us to examine how we are spending our lives as Christians lest much (if not all) that we are involved in should be burned up as wood, hay and stubble on the last day.

Some penetrating questions now need to be answered:

1. How much of my life can only be explained in terms of God, since it has no human explanation? How much of the corporate life of my church can only be explained in terms of God—since it is beyond human explanation?

2. Do I really want what I read about in Acts to be part of my life and the life of the fellowship to which I belong, recognizing that Paul's first miracle was one of hurting not of healing, and church members dropped dead because of the way they handled the collection?

3. Am I prepared to trust the unpredictable control

of the Holy Spirit, who can do anything he wants to because he is God—and often he will if I would only let him? It will always be for good, but constantly surprising.

4. Am I prepared for the cost of all this—the cost of allowing God to have first place in my life? The effect on my career, my lifestyle, my security and my money will be profound.

I suppose the overriding question that remains on reading the twenty-eight chapters of the Acts of the Apostles is not just, 'Do I believe what I read there?' but, 'Do I want that to be my experience of life?'

8

Reach for the Sky!

Out of the twenty-eight chapters of the Acts of the Apostles twenty mention prayer and many of these are a record of effective and challenging praying. One of the men in our church, to whom God has given a very significant pastoring gift and combined it effectively with a gift of teaching, was teaching in our Bible school one Sunday morning. He said: 'Prayer is not so much moving God into our world to solve our problems, as it is God moving us into his world to serve his purposes.' I had been away for the weekend and was listening to the tape of this teaching on my return. All that he said was helpful and spiritually nourishing, but this little comment ministered life to me and verbalized a new perspective of prayer for me.

I don't know whether it was an original thought that God had put into Gordon's heart, or whether it was something he had received from elsewhere and it had become real to him. That does not really matter, for all I do know is that I have returned to this again and again, for prayer is not me getting God to do what I want; nor is it God getting me to do what he wants. Prayer is me getting God to do what he wants. God wants us to know where he is going and then to join him. You may say that God will do that anyway—but that does not appear to be so, because the Bible indicates that 'you do not have because you do not ask'. I am required to pray and in doing so I hold the door open to God to go through and so into situations where he can fulfil his purposes. For prayer touches three worlds at one time: prayer touches heaven and God as nothing else can; prayer touches earth and affects man at a depth and a reality as nothing else will; and prayer touches hell and disturbs the devil more than any other human enterprise.

Quite clearly in Acts prayer was an invitation received to experience and explore the boundlessness of God. It was never regarded as a way of escape, but the grasping of the offer of a way of victory. It was conquest and not evasion. It provided the enabling of God to confront the hard and dangerous thing, and delivered these early Christians from the constant temptation to find a way round it. They did not avoid the difficulty, but accepted it and overcame it. As devout Jews they knew that prayer was God's idea and not something which had emerged from an evangelical conference or a well-meaning church committee which had spent endless hours deliberating for many months. God had said: 'Call to me, and I will answer you: I will tell you wonderful and marvellous things that you know nothing about' (Jer 33:3)—and they were thrilled by this. They were thrilled enough to believe it and then do it.

They realized that God the Father was involved as soon as they prayed—because he was listening. They also appreciated that God the Son was involved—because he pleaded on their behalf before the Father. They certainly appreciated that God the Holy Spirit was involved—because he helped them get going by influencing their minds and their mouths. They were aware that they had two helpers when they prayed to the Father—one in heaven speaking on their behalf and one on earth stimulating their prayers. 'It must be remembered,' writes William Barclay, 'that the prayer which finds God is one of the most strenuous activities which the spirit of man can undertake.' So strenuous, indeed, that the spirit of man is impotent and inadequate unless invaded by the Spirit of God. Albert Edward Day, in his book, *Existence under God,* describes this true prayer:

> It is not merely a flash of Godward drive, but the passionate fervour of a whole self that pants to know God and His will above all other knowing. It is not the hurried visit to the window of a religious drive-in restaurant for a moral sandwich or a cup of spiritual stimulant, but an unhurried communion with God who is never in a hurry. It is not merely the expression of a transient mood of dependence or loneliness, but the consistent cry of one who seeks to perceive and express the Ultimate Beauty. It is the antithesis of dilly-dally devotions, drowsy murmurs from a pillow where sleep lies in wait, the lazy lisping of familiar phrases that should shake one to the core of one's being. It is the find-or-die outreach of the soul for God.[17]

The great tragedy of so much of our activity is that it is ineffective in accomplishing the real purposes of God. Most of us know what it feels like to live so crowded a life that there is scarcely a moment to spare, and yet at the end of the day we have so little, if anything at all, to show for it. Vast tracts of our lives, both personally and corporately, are untouched by prayer!

Acts is permeated by the spirit and practice of prayer which recognizes that prayer is to the Father, through the Son and in the Spirit, but it is also against the devil and with the saints. This is the ultimate in spiritual warfare and also in the experience of Christian fellowship. So the power of God is released, not to destroy, but to create, not to spawn despair, but to give birth to hope in the darkest situation; not to be negative, but to be positive; not for death, but for life. It is the opportunity to think God's thoughts, feel God's emotions, desire God's plan, speak God's words and do God's works—even in a seemingly impossible position.

There has been considerable controversy over the years about *when* the church was born. Some have said the church was born in eternity—since it has always been in the heart and mind of God. Others have felt that its origins can be dated back to Adam in the Garden of Eden, since he was the first created being on earth to worship God and have fellowship with him. Again others have traced the church's origin to the time of Abraham, that eighty-year-old father of the faithful, who left the advanced civilization of Ur, with its centrally-heated houses and running water in the bedrooms, to live in a tent. Still others see the church's initiation at the time of Moses, who led God's people out of slavery into freedom—and indeed the first time the word 'church' (the congregation or company of God's people) appears in the Bible is when Israel is in the wilderness of Sinai. Undoubtedly Jesus was making a clear statement about the failure of Israel in fulfilling the purposes of God and the need to make a new beginning when he called twelve men to be his disciples. This was a new community of believers—a new Israel. However, the day of Pentecost (Acts 2) was clearly 'blast-off day' so far as the church is concerned. On that remarkable occasion the motors were ignited and the church was sent into orbit as the power of God fell on that unusual and unlikely group of 120 men and women.

However, if there is controversy over *when* the

church began, there is no denying *how* the church began—it began in the climate of prayer (Acts 1:4). These men and women had witnessed the ascension of Jesus and realized that he had gone to heaven in his resurrection body. Little did they realize that God desired and required a new body on earth to declare his word and demonstrate his power, and that they were to be part—indeed members—of that new body, the church. They spent the ten-day period between the drama of the ascension and the event of Pentecost in a prayer-meeting.

Significantly it was when Jesus had been baptized and he was praying (Lk 3:21) that God anointed his incarnate body—the first body of Christ on earth. God immediately reminded him of who he was—a royal Son—as he spoke out of heaven from a coronation psalm which Jesus, as a Jew by birth and upbringing, would have immediately recognized (Ps 2). At the same time God reminded his Son how he was to fulfil his mission and ministry. He was to be the servant, who came not to be served, but to serve and to give (Is 40). Jesus again must have quickly realized the implication of one of the great 'servant' passages from the prophecy of Isaiah which his Father was using.

How often we need to be reminded who we are—royal children of the King, and yet always servants owned by him and used as he desires. Clearly prayer is not only the climate in which God works to fulfil his purposes, but it is the soil out of which good plants will grow and good fruit will be produced. It is an exercise so contrary to our flesh, and so powerfully opposed to and effective against the devil, that we are reluctant to invest time and energy in it, since we are persuaded that a multitude of other things are more relevant and effective in our lives and in our service as citizens of the kingdom of God.

Acts 2:43-47 has often been held up to us (and it ought to be) as the exciting, challenging, compelling picture of the church as God always intended it to be. Acts 2:1-4 must always issue in Acts 2:43-47. Pentecost was, and continues to be, God's response to the weakness and ineptitude of Christian believers. God intended to transform us—by the power of his Spirit—into an effective, unified, rejoicing company of his servants who could and would demonstrate his power and declare his word. We have often been entranced by the five characteristics of the first appearance of this new phenomenon on earth—the church of the living God. They were a church in which *reverence* permeated all that they did—'everyone was filled with awe' (Acts 2:43). God requires a godly fear in his people, since only then can they begin to see things from his point of view. This is neither a cowering terror nor an unhealthy phobia. It is the natural reaction of the human personality to the realization of who God really is. This was inevitable for them, since the supernatural was normal among them—'many miracles and wonders were being done through the apostles'. They experienced an immanence of God which is sometimes found in individuals these days but seldom in a corporate group of Christians.

The next thing which is impressive about this newly-born, infant church is that from day one they achieved a remarkable level of *sharing*: 'All the believers continued together in close fellowship and shared their belongings with one another. They would sell their property and possessions, and distribute the money among all, according to what each needed.' This was neither an imposed regulation nor a mandatory directive, but a spontaneous, voluntary reaction to the new spiritual reality which flowed within them and among them. Expressing a not dissimilar attitude, Admiral

Lord Nelson, when congratulated about one of his notable exploits at sea, replied: 'I had the happiness to command a band of brothers.'

A third characteristic of the new church was a simple, unaffected *consistency*. They were apparently just as happy praising God in their homes as they were in the Temple: 'Day after day they met as a group in the Temple, and they had their meals together in their homes, eating with glad and humble hearts, praising God.' They had breached that artificial and restrictive barrier which creates a division between the sacred and the secular. Such a distinction no longer existed. Again there was *reality* in what they were about—they were 'enjoying the goodwill of all the people'. Sometimes (not always!) the charge of hypocrisy and escapism and unreality is justified in the contemporary church. Here, however, there was the impact of something which was desirable and real upon a word-proof, struggling, bewildered society. What they saw in the church appealed to them. Whether they wanted to go the way necessary to get it for themselves is another matter. There was a marked absence of the gloominess, tenseness and conformity which characterizes so much church life today —and society liked it!

Finally, this church was a *growing* church—it was an organism rather than an organization. 'And every day the Lord added to their group those who were being saved' (Acts 2:47). We need to note, 'every day'. There was nothing static about this new, living thing which had appeared under the hand of God and as a result of the ministry of the Holy Spirit. Generally this has been the case throughout the church's history—and today the church worldwide is growing more rapidly than at any other time in her history. It is estimated that another seventeen Christians are born into the family of God every minute. A friend of mine—a minister—

was attending a function held for businessmen. Someone there asked him—rather rudely, I think—'What is it like to belong to a dying organization?' 'I would not know!' he replied. Unhappily we do not always see, nor do we always expect to see a growth development locally in the church.

It is easy to be attracted to these five characteristics of the Acts church, but we need at the same time to acknowledge how they were achieved. There are five causes which give rise to these five consequences. These five causes are concisely contained in Acts 2:37-42.

First of all, each of the individuals who comprised this church underwent a personal spiritual revolution. They had come to realize their spiritual destitution before God—no matter how they were regarded locally by society nor what position they had within it. So far as spiritual reality was concerned they were lost, completely out of fellowship with the God for whom they had been made, careering towards a disintegrating eternity, and totally without hope in the world. The Spirit of God had prepared their hearts to recognize that there was now only one course of action open to them—to repent! That would affect how they thought, how they felt, what they said, and what they did. Their *baptism in water* (Acts 2:38) was no subscription to some credal statement, but the outward, overt expression of the deep reality within their hearts. They had experienced spiritual crucifixion, and death demanded burial to follow. Such was the experience of baptism for them. But the gospel they received was not simply a means for dealing with sin, but also the means for equipping them for relevant living, and so baptism in water was accompanied by *baptism in the Holy Spirit.* The church became the vital, vibrant thing we see in Acts because it began in simplicity and reality. There is no trace here of nominal formality. The corporate group comprised individuals into whose lives God had come in a powerful way, convincing them that Jesus is Lord and challenging them to live his risen life in the power of the Holy Spirit. Entrance into life in the kingdom did not so much enrich the human family as it ensured life in the family of God.

The second cause of these dynamic consequences was that they had teachable spirits—they were willing to *learn* what they were *taught.* Luke says, 'They spent their time in learning from the apostles.' All of them came from a tradition where teaching and learning were important ingredients in life. Belief and behaviour were not rooted in heady concepts, but in the flesh and blood of human history and the mystical authority of divine revelation. As Jews they were clearly instructed in what had happened in the past and why, and at the same time in what would happen in the future, although when that would be was not so certain. Many of their traditions were now challenged with truth from the word of God. Tradition can so easily give way to prejudice, but it is not so with truth. The apostles' concern was to hear what God was saying through his word. It was for this reason that they initiated the office of deacon (Acts 6:1-7) because the pressure of circumstances was intruding so much on their time that their teaching ministry was becoming seriously endangered. It is not that they were graduate material (indeed the facts seem to suggest that nothing could have been further from the truth), but they were open to God to teach them all that he wanted them to know to enable them to live God-honouring lives. So there was not only a *spiritual* cause, but also an *educational* cause.

Yet another aspect of this was a *social* cause. They did not just do the same things together, they shared the same things together. *Fellowship* was enjoyed and experienced at a level that we know little of in the Western church. It was not simply the expression of a friendly greeting or an interested comment, but the vulnerability to lay life open before one's brethren for encouragement, guidance and affirmation, or for rebuke and correction. This was a completely new dimension in human relationships. It demanded a trust and commitment to one another at a depth which could only be achieved supernaturally. Where the contemporary church has tried to follow the lead of the early church in this area of fellowship without the dynamic of the Spirit there have been many disasters.

Closely allied to this third cause was a willingness to share their food together. They came out of a tradition where *eating* often had the element of celebration about it. It need not be elaborate, but the implications of eating together were profound. Within contemporary society eating has been reduced to a functional necessity. It is prepared with an ever-increasing rapidity and consumed often in the same spirit. Sometimes we even seem to go out of our way not to relate when we eat, as we sit in rows facing a wall rather than one another. It is significant that a great deal of the ministry of Jesus took place around a meal.

The final ingredient which gave rise to such a notable effect was that they 'took part in . . . prayers'. It seems to be that they used the synagogue and Temple *prayers*. These were part of their heritage and had impressed themselves deeply upon them through the impressionable years into maturity. However, what they had recited, parrot-fashion, for years now became life and reality as the Spirit of God touched them. The set, liturgical prayer provided the framework from which there flowed great freedom as they explored the boundlessness and the bounty of the purposes of God. This was no dead structure, but a thrilling, living reality.

So the church continued to grow and develop. Peter and John (Acts 3:1) 'went to the Temple at three o'clock in the afternoon, the hour for prayer' without hesitancy or criticism. This was the natural routine of those who had been filled with the Holy Spirit. They did not despise what they might have regarded now as dead structure, nor did they criticize it. They involved themselves in it as those who knew reality in their religion.

There is almost an inevitability about it that when the first devastating wave of persecution crashed upon them and they were forbidden to preach by law and, on pain of severe punishment, warned by the authorities not to speak publicly about Jesus or minister or heal in his name—they prayed. When we pray God joins in. The evidence of his presence on this occasion was frighteningly dramatic: 'When they finished praying, the place where they were meeting was shaken.' God shook the building as a reminder that they were in his hands. Centuries later, when he was confronted and terrorized by the authority of Rome, and the Pope said to Martin Luther, 'Martin Luther, where will you be when I have done all this to you?' Luther replied: 'I will be where I have always been—in the hands of God.' Then, as here in Acts, God was powerfully saying to his followers and dependants, 'You do not need to worry about these people—I have a hold of the church.' To underline his care and control he gave these pressurized Christians another Pentecost experience. I have never personally been at a prayer meeting like this, but I realize I can learn from their attitude to prayer and the content of their prayers on this occasion (Acts 4:23-30).

They began not in complaint or panic, but by getting a big view of God—'Master and Creator of heaven, earth, and sea, and all that is in them!' Most of our spiritual problems are caused because our practical view of God is too small. We sometimes have a small view of God and a big view of ourselves. Often we have a small view of God and a small view of ourselves—a sure recipe for spiritual impotence and personal capitulation. Occasionally we have a big view of God and a small view of ourselves—and we have confused humility with unreality. But God longs to give us a big view of himself and a big view of ourselves. One of the most serious maladies the contemporary church faces is a loss of personal identity among its members. We have often lost sight of who we are as Christians. We are loved and chosen by God. God knows us—and has done so through eternity—and loves us and wants us just the same. He gave his Son to die for us and his Spirit to fill us. He has gifted us so that we would be real and relevant people for the fulfilling of his purposes. He watches over us in time and wants us to spend eternity with him. We need not only a big practical view of God, but a big practical view of ourselves, so that we can stand up again when the crashing waves of opposition would destroy us, and with head erect and eyes shining walk with confidence into the future—by prayer. These early Christians fed on the Scriptures in prayer (Ps 2:1-2). The word of God ministered confidence into them. The impact of what they were reminded of was: 'These people are silly to set themselves against you—for whether it is in past history or present circumstances, God is in charge.' It is so encouraging these days to lift the newspaper and read its doleful catalogue of darkness and duplicity and disaster and know with great certainty: 'God, you are in charge!'

With this confidence these early Christians no longer cried for protection or preservation, but for boldness to speak God's message and see God's miracles: 'Allow us, your servants, to speak your message with all boldness. Reach out your hand to heal, and grant that wonders and miracles may be performed through the name of your holy servant Jesus.' They recognized their weakness and proneness to compromise, and opened their hearts to God about it. Their constant cry to God was for courage—the boldness to do it right. God's response was immediate and dramatic. It is difficult for us to be confident that when we really pray God joins in. In fact, we need to realize that when we pray—no matter how alone we may feel—we are never alone. In fact the place of prayer can get quite crowded. The Father is listening; the Son is interceding; and the Spirit is right beside us on earth enabling. The hosts of heaven are interested and involved, and the powers of darkness are roused to attack and oppose. Prayer wakes the response of a great unseen multitude.

Most exciting of all is that God joins in. As in Acts 4:31, so in Acts 16:25-26. It was about midnight and 'Paul and Silas were praying and singing hymns to God' and again God stepped in and 'there was a violent earthquake, which shook the prison to its foundations. At once all the doors opened, and the chains fell off all the prisoners'. Clearly God was in control. Where have you ever heard of an earthquake which opens doors (it normally crushes and traps rather than opens and frees); loosens every chain without hurting anyone; and causes great rejoicing? This was clearly not a natural event, but a supernatural one. God gives us two profound insights in Acts 16. One is that in God's thinking good and evil are to be kept apart (16:16-21)—although the world wants to join them. The other is that in God's thinking the natural and the supernatural are to be kept together (16:22-40)—although the world insists on separating them.

Acts 16 is a salutary reminder that it is futile to imagine that when you become a Christian everything is now going to be smooth-running and straightforward.

However, it is a reminder also that when trouble breaks in upon us there are no grounds for us being daunted and falling into dark despair—we can triumph in trouble. We need to learn how to pray and praise in such a way that God joins in. Two of the greatest misconceptions of the Christian life are that it is possible to be a Christian without prayer and, secondly, that it will always be a pleasant, and convenient experience. The corporate prayer meetings which are recorded in Acts present us with two realistic options—a dimension of God and his presence which is to be coveted with a holy greed, although the effect may well be unexpectedly alarming—for example, a baptism in the Holy Spirit resulting in exultant worship in an unlearned language and powerful, relevant witnessing (Acts 2:14); a whole building physically shaking (Acts 4:31); an earthquake which drove a normally balanced, stable Roman citizen to the point of suicide (Acts 16:27). The other option is a dull, routine formality which expects little and usually gets less than it expects.

Acts is not merely the only history book of the New Testament, but it is also a powerful record of the spread of the gospel of Christ effectively into society. Each new thrust is formed in the context of prayer. It is when he is praying (9:11) that God is preparing the apostle Paul for his great task of taking the transforming grace of God in Christ to the gentiles—ardent and vindictive Jew though he was. This was God's message to the astonished and hesitant Ananias: 'Go, because I have chosen him to serve me, to make my name known to the Gentiles and kings and to the people of Israel. And I myself will show him all that he must suffer for my sake' (Acts 9:15-16). Paul recalls this vivid prayer experience as he gives his testimony in his defence (Acts 22:17-21).

It was within the context of routine, regular praying

(Acts 10:1-3) that God had his opportunity to unveil his heart to Cornelius and so initiate the accomplishment of his eternal purposes. It was to another—Peter, a Jew—that God continued to reveal his purposes of including the Gentiles in his salvation. Again it was during the experience of prayer (Acts 10:9). Peter is given a very dramatic vision of an opened heaven and a tense conversation follows between the Lord and his servant in which his prejudice and inflexible thinking are deeply challenged. The key to the whole record is the dawning realization that 'God treats everyone on the same basis' and 'whoever fears him and does what is right is acceptable to him no matter what race he belongs to' (Acts 10:34-35). Undoubtedly even now the biggest problem of the human race is not disease or even death, but bitter prejudice. How many crimes of callous viciousness have been perpetrated on this thinly disguised basis it would be hard to estimate. But it was in prayer that God was able to grapple with this destructive human symptom. The connection between prejudice and prayerlessness is close and strong inside as well as outside the church. There are few greater hindrances and handicaps to the gospel of Christ than traditional, irrational and deeply subconscious prejudice. Praying (as we have already noticed) moves us into God's world to fulfil his purposes rather than us moving God into our world to strengthen our prejudices.

It was in prayer that the dynamic for extending the church through Asia Minor exploded and the initiation of the preaching tour of Galatia was born (12:25-16:5), resulting in the churches being 'made stronger in the faith and growing in numbers every day' (16:5). This happened while an extraordinary group of people were at prayer—Barnabas, a Cypriot with generous hand and head; Simeon, a black African who had carried the cross of Jesus on Good Friday; Lucius, a Roman; Manaen, brought up in a palace and foster-brother to prince Herod; and Saul, a Benjamite Jew from Tarsus, trained as a Rabbi and previously a persecutor of the young church. It is a mixture of race, religious background, class and culture united in a common conviction that God is real, and his reality is demonstrated in that he responds to the cry of the human heart and reveals his purposes to the sons of men.

They were not only an extraordinary group of men, but they met in an extraordinarily hostile climate. Antioch is about a hundred miles north of Galilee and enjoyed a notorious reputation because of its ritual prostitution and flamboyant night life. It is almost certain that this is the place Jesus had in mind when he spoke of the prodigal son going into 'the far country'. The church here has been described as a 'cluster of chaste snowdrops growing on a foul rubbish heap'. In this place these men denied their physical appetite to stimulate their spiritual appetite. They exemplified that fasting and praying were partners. They were 'serving' *(leitourgounton)* the Lord in the sense that they were worshipping him and waiting on him. It is from this word that we get our word 'liturgy'. It is in this activity and attitude that God gives the Christians in Antioch staggering information which disturbed them—'I want your two best members!' Speaking on behalf of overseas missions, Michael Griffiths reminds us that this is always God's way. Michael says to the 'home' church, 'If you don't miss them, we don't want them.' So Asia Minor too was opened up to the gospel out of a prayer context.

It was also in prayer that God opened up the prospect of taking the gospel into a totally new continent—Europe. In some senses, in view of his immediate past, it was a small step for Paul, but it was a gigantic step for

Christianity. Europe was to become the radiating centre for Christianity during the next 2,000 years. Paul's relationship with and response to the Lord shows two important principles which are relevant to our praying—the principle of the shut door and the principle of the moving object. Sometimes we think we know the way forward, and we are filled with excitement, enthusiasm and anticipation as a result—only to find that that way is blocked by a closed door. It is tragically easy to be so absorbed by the shut door that we completely miss the door that God is going to open. Paul was prevented by the Holy Spirit from preaching in Asia Minor, and was led instead to go to Macedonia in mainland Europe (Acts 16:6-9). Paul handled the principle of the shut door well, and so must we.

This section of the exciting unfolding of God's purpose to and through a human life is a powerful reminder too of the principle of the moving object. Physicists tell us that it is much easier to change the direction of a moving body than a static one. Paul had an active not a passive view of guidance. Prayer 'on the hoof' as we pursue the will of God actively is likely to succeed.

It must be because it is so powerful and relevant an activity and so spiritually real that our enemy who reigns in the kingdom of darkness uses every possible means—subtle and obvious—to waylay us as we move towards prayer. Many of us within the church know all the powerful arguments for prayer, and we have explored the convincing evidence that should make us eager to pray—and yet we do not do it.

To put it at its most basic level, although Christian prayer is quite *distinctive,* it is *instinctive.* Human beings are not just animals, although Desmond Morris has written extensively in *The Naked Ape* and *The Human Zoo* to show animal feelings in human beings.

(Johnny Morris, on the other hand, looks very entertainingly at animals and projects human feelings onto them!) It is true that we share much with the animal kingdom—we breathe the same air, have comparable digestive and reproductive systems in our bodies—but we are not animals. We, the human race, have sunk to depths of cruelty and sadism that the animal kingdom has never sunk to. It is inaccurate, and often a disservice to the animals, to speak about *'bestial'* behaviour in people. However, it is equally true that we humans rise to heights animals can never achieve.

What is the basic difference between mankind and the animal world? Man is not distinctive in that he talks—for even fish communicate in a very basic fashion. Nor is he distinctive because he makes tools—for so do the chimpanzees. To the best of our knowledge the animal kingdom has never discovered nor used fire. Nor do the animals laugh—although the hyena gives a very good imitation of human laughter! But there is a fundamental difference between man and the animals—man prays. Even the simplest and most primitive man prays. Never is man more distinctively human than when he prays. At some time and in certain circumstances—however irreligious he may be, and however apparently godless his lifestyle—a man will pray. So prayer is instinctive to the human being. Prayer, however, is quite distinctive for Christian man. It is not the same for him to be on his knees as it is for the Tibetan monk to be revolving his prayer wheel or the Muslim prostrating himself at certain times in the day, facing Mecca. There are unique and profound differences between ordinary prayer and Christian prayer.

Christian prayer is to our heavenly Father—who really exists, and knows my name. He is one who hears and listens, replies and acts when I cry out to him.

Christian prayer is also through the Son. There is One in heaven who knows what it is like to be on earth—and he is interceding before the Father on my behalf. But Christian prayer not only has help in heaven, but also on earth, because the Holy Spirit comes alongside me to encourage, enlighten and enable me as soon as I will to pray. Every time the Christian prays he is engaging in an assault against the devil. The kingdom of darkness has little concern for prayerless living and serving. But prayerful activity excites a ready response from it. With Christian praying there is another distinctive feature—it is never really possible to pray alone. Apart from the Son of God being involved in heaven in our praying and the Spirit of God being involved on earth in our praying, the angels get involved with us as we pray. And frequently other Christians want to get involved with us when we pray.

Just over a year ago a very dear friend of mine—who prayed for me daily—went to be with the Lord. I have missed her more than I could ever express. Indifferent health and a frail body restricted her movements and active participation in all kinds of things that were very dear to her heart, but as her physical robustness declined she engaged in spiritual battle with awesome effect. Only heaven has been able to record the full impact. From time to time, with a straightforward simplicity, God would speak to her not only personally, but also for our church to which she belonged. Very shortly before she died God spoke through her in this way:

> My people, why do you not pray? What are you waiting for? If you will only assemble together I will show you how to pray. I want simplicity; I want reality in your praying.
>
> As you grow in expectancy, so will I give revelation. But wait for it and expect it. Assemble yourselves together. Be still and do not be afraid of silence—because I am in it,

and I love you. Be still and know that I am God. Be still and know that I am here. I will speak to you when you are ready—so be still, wait and listen. Be willing to learn from me.

My people, why are you not responding in prayer? I have called you to prayer. I am waiting.

God used one of his frail, gentle servants to bring this word to us. Her life was the embodiment of the mingled strength and gentleness of God. It is so like God to use one like this to express the cry of his own heart. That cry was specifically for us as a congregation—and yet also for the whole church in the West perhaps!

9

Into Battle

God has called us not only to be his sons and servants, but also to be his soldiers. Two great misconceptions have bedevilled the Western church. One is that Christianity is *possible* — we have learned how to 'do it'. We have built our structures and traditions so that as long as we abide within them and follow them all is well. We are no longer exposed regularly to the unexpected and the impossible. Routine has eliminated the unexpected and theology has dealt with the impossible. The other great misconception is that to be a Christian is *pleasant*. That has often been the emphasis of the gospel we have preached. Hardship, pain and the unattractive have often been soft-pedalled, muted and even ignored altogether. Garibaldi, who gave himself to the unification and liberation of Italy, never made any bones about what was involved: 'I promise you forced marches, short rations, bloody battles, wounds, imprisonment, and death—but let him who loves home and fatherland follow me.' And men followed him—and history records their daring and was shaped by them.

The Acts story is full of records of men and women who had given up the idea that Christianity was difficult—they recognized it was totally impossible (apart from the grace and the invasion of God). They never understood it to be a pleasant Sunday morning or evening exercise, but a painful experience that intruded—often violently—into every area of their lives both privately and publicly, personally and corporately. There was a rapid dawning upon them that the gospel was not simply a biography of Jesus—it was not simply God's story or even a good story. It was a call to enlistment. Many Christians imagine they are civilians. They are not—they are soldiers. We are not living in peacetime, but in wartime.

In the gospel of Mark there is nothing about either the birth or the boyhood of Jesus. Mark deals with three years of Jesus' life—not thirty-three years. One third of what he writes has to do with Jesus' death. The Victorians were obsessed with death—maybe because they confronted it so often—and recorded very detailed and often dramatic death-bed scenes, but they never highlighted it to that enormous proportion. In Mark's view the gospel was a battle which had been fought and a war whose outcome was now never in doubt. Often in the Roman Empire there was a war going on far away from Rome. In the city of Rome they waited with bated breath for news of the battles which were being fought. When a battle was won, a messenger was despatched to Rome, and as he approached the gates of the city he shouted, 'Good news! Good news! Good news!' or, in our terms, 'Gospel! Gospel! Gospel!' It meant that victory had been secured in the battle. Particularly, then, in the gospel of Mark the author is saying by implication, 'I am going to write about a war and how the crucial battle has been fought and won. However difficult and dangerous the remainder of the war is, be assured that victory will never be in doubt and peace will come.' In the Second World War many casualties occurred between D-Day and VE-Day, but after D-Day the outcome was never in doubt.

Superficially, in the gospel it looks like a war between Jesus and the Jews. The Jews were his constant opponents and consistently challenged and condemned what he said and did, and often considered and planned ways to remove him. It is a remarkable evidence of how Satan—the enemy of both God and men—will utilize the most unlikely people for his purposes. After all, Jesus was a Jew, and yet his own earthly kinsmen were the most severe on him. The Jews were godly people as a race in the time of Jesus. The Pharisees who were so often the sharp end of the opposition were devoutly religious—they prayed more frequently than most do in the contemporary Western church; they knew their Scriptures with an intimacy and detail which eludes the average church leader today; they gave their money to God with a consistency and in proportion to their earnings that would put the ordinary church member to shame. These were the people who consistently tried to frustrate the mission of Jesus. But the war that Jesus fought was not against the Jews. Nor was it a conflict between good and evil. It was a direct confrontation between God and Satan.

Jesus won—and the fruits of his victory are there for us to enjoy. Unfortunately we live as a race under the tyranny of the same enemy Jesus fought. He has convinced us that we are unable ever to be free, although 'the Son of God appeared for this very reason to destroy what the devil had done' (1 Jn 3:8; GNB, adapted). After the Slavery Act had been clearly put on the statute books by the British Parliament, declaring that slavery was now illegal wherever the British Government had authority, there were many who continued to exercise a slavery hold over men and women and even more who accepted it. Thousands of slaves did not know they were free now, and lived under the tyranny of their masters. Their freedom had been secured, but no one had told them so. As with social and political slavery, so it is spiritually—millions in this country and across the world do not know they are free because of who Jesus was and what Jesus did.

It is well that we stop thinking of the enemy of the kingdom of God as an outdated, simplistic concept. Significantly, there is a dearth of references to the demonic in the Old Testament. We need to wait until we arrive at the gospel narratives of the New Testament to see that Satan and his demons are in a full-scale war with Jesus. The demonic appears most profusely when Jesus is present—and that continues to be so. When Jesus is present among us today in the person and power of his Holy Spirit—then the enemy will manifest himself in one way or another. When Jesus appears the kingdom of darkness is directly threatened and a commotion results on earth (Mk 1:21-28). The kingdom of God was and is present in Jesus (Mt 12:28), and he has broken the power of their control in human lives. Their influence is thoroughly demonstrated in the New Testament. The key to this was and is the presence of the kingdom of God. Significantly, when the new body of Christ appears on earth, the kingdom of darkness emerges obtrusively.

The devil cannot be dismissed as 'old smutty face' or displayed as a red, grotesque figure with a forked tail, a trident in his hand and a leer on his face. Our concepts of him often come from the frightened architecture of the Middle Ages or the poetic pages of Milton's *Paradise Lost* rather than the revelation of Scripture or the real encounters that men and women have with him. During the Second World War, Field Marshal Bernard Montgomery achieved his victory over the German army in the North African desert largely as a result of his painstaking study of his opponent, Field Marshal Rommel. He studied his character, his temperament, his personal habits, and his tactics in previous battles. He even had a photograph of him in his desert caravan.

The Bible never makes light of the one who opposes us as we would walk individually and together in righteousness. He is *Satan* — the accuser and slanderer, who accuses and slanders God to us and us to God. He is the *vanisher,* who convinces us that he does not really exist. So adept is he at this that when the Convocation of Canterbury and York were debating a new Catechism in 1963 this parliament of the Church of England just 'squeezed' the devil in at the last moment, since many were questioning whether he really existed. Many unenlightened (although curiously enough they regard themselves as enlightened) churches today do not believe in the existence of Satan and consequently are lifeless and powerless.

He is the *angel of light*—the shining one, the lightbearer, Lucifer. He often comes pretending to be God —interrupting our devotional life and impressing his perverted direction for our lives through the most unlikely human beings. He is the *father of lies,* utilizing truth, but making a lie of it—often not by what he says, but by what he leaves unsaid. He is the *serpent,* calling in question the clearly stated and heard word of God. He is the *accuser,* pointing remorselessly and accurately to past sin in the believer and always omitting the reality that sin no longer clings to him, for on the basis of the believer's repentance towards God Jesus has cleansed him.

Satan is the *god of this world,* where he exercises his greatest success through secular philosophies which have a direct bearing upon the way that we live our lives. He is the *ruler of the kingdom of the air,* spawning all contemporary godless philosophies, religions and culturally derived perceptions of life which are not biblical in their source. He is the *prince of this world*, usurping the individual's right and ability to live in freedom and making him a prisoner in his domain. Wherever the individual, through sin, yields his right to free choice, he places himself in bondage to the prince of this world. It was Jesus, facing up to all the pain and pressures of our humanity yet never sinning, who could say with a childlike assurance, 'The ruler of this world is coming. He has no power over me . . .' (Jn 14:30).

Henry Law, from an earlier generation, gives us a powerful description of the devil's ceaseless activity against us:

> He never slumbers, never is weary, never relents, never abandons hope. He deals his blows alike at childhood's weakness, youth's inexperience, manhood's strength, and the totterings of age. He watches to ensnare the morning thought, he departs not with the shades of night. . . . He enters the palace, the hut, the fortress, the camp, the fleet. He invades every chamber of every dwelling, every pew of every sanctuary. He is busy with the busy. He hurries about with the active. He sits by each bed of sickness and whispers into each dying ear. As the spirit quits the tenement of clay, he still draws his bow with unrelenting rage.

There are at least twelve characteristics of Satan's strategy that need to be noted, as he aims to gain dominance over the whole person of the human being. He wants to control and manipulate us spiritually; to afflict us physically (e.g. Mt 9:32-33; 12:22; Mk 9:14-19); to deceive us mentally (Gen 3:1-5; Acts 5:3); to disturb us emotionally (2 Tim 1:7); and delude us doctrinally (1 Tim 4:1-3; 1 Jn 4:1-2).

Satan *attacks* us viciously (1 Pet 5:8). He is not only portrayed as the king of the beasts, but he is hungry and determined to satisfy himself by devouring us. Strength and destructiveness are aspects of his attacks. Often his approach is brutal. He *takes advantage* of weakness (2 Cor 2:11). He will be strongest and most intrusive when we are behaving and reacting in the most human way—when we excuse our unacceptable behaviour and reactions as being natural. He *blinds* the human mind and understanding from having any kind of spiritual perception (2 Cor 4:4). So men see truth and call it a lie and confront light and call it darkness. They become aware of right and call it wrong, and perceive wrong and call it right.

He provides a *counterfeit* to reality (Acts 8:9-11). He will attempt to reproduce what God is doing so that the gullible will be taken in by his wiles. Having enticed us, he will then undoubtedly ensnare us. His stock-in-trade is *deception* (Rev 12:9). His field of operation stretches across the whole world and attempts to invade every situation. He *hinders* the gospel (2 Thess 2:7-10) by getting people enamoured by the lies which he tells and the miracles which he performs. Engrossed in his darkness, the light comes and is not received.

He *steals* the truth (Mt 13:19). He is never more active than when God is on the move. He does not operate in territory which is separate from where God is at work. Where there is a work of God, either individually or corporately, the enemy is at work with a frightening enthusiasm. So what God gives he quickly wants to remove or destroy. He *afflicts* and *destroys* (Jn 10:10). He is a vandal. He never comes to create—only to confuse. He never comes to build up—only to tear down. He never comes to enhance—only to mock. He *indwells* the physical frame (Mt 8:31 ff.). Animals as well as men become the targets of his tenancy. He is always on the hunt for a place to live. Such must be our concern that neither consciously nor inadvertently do we give him room and board. As the father of lies he *lies* (Acts 5:3). He made Ananias and Sapphira a mortal danger to the newly-born church because of their pretence and hypocrisy. They pretended to be what they were not. It was not what they gave or what they withheld which created the problem—it was their deception which introduced corruption and death into that young fellowship.

He *opposes* the angels of God (Zech 3:1). Only eternity will reveal the awesome battle which has gone on in the heavenlies. On earth we know only a side-skirmish of that conflict. He *tempts* God's children to sin (Lk 22:31). It was not just Simon Peter that he wanted to have, but all of those called by Jesus: 'Simon, Simon! Listen! Satan has received permission to test all of you.' The 'you' here is plural in its form and refers not to one, but to all.

We have frequently lost sight of these facts about the enemy in the contemporary church and in our common life. Yet to examine the ministry of Jesus is to be aware of the activity of Satan. A quarter of Jesus' ministry is devoted to handling overt demonic activity and securing freedom through deliverance for those who had become ensnared and enslaved. Having been baptized in water and anointed by the Holy Spirit, Jesus is immediately led by the Holy Spirit to a desert place to enter into a direct confrontation with Satan. Clearly it was the intention of God to enable his Son to be aware of what he was up against and who his real enemy was and where his real opposition would come from. All of this had to be confronted right away. The tests that he underwent are all tests a Spirit-filled Christian must handle (Mt 4:1-11).

Jesus was pressurized to see whether he would use divine resources for building the kingdom of God for his own personal needs. The second temptation was to push him to confuse foolishness with faith. How easily the enemy will quote Scripture to us and blind us to the whole counsel of God. He did it then and he continues to do so today—often with sad and confusing results. The third temptation to which he was subjected was confrontation with the real—not fictional—possibility of taking a short cut to achieve what he came to do by recognizing the devil's authority. The seductive thought that the end justifies the means is never very far away from us and when these circumstances present themselves to us, it is never easy to resist. So self-interest, confusing faith with foolishness and fantasy, and achieving our goal by illegitimate means are all temptations which have got to be resisted.

Satan was in the business of destroying Jesus from the very beginning of his emerging ministry. Had he succeeded, the cross and the atoning death of our Saviour would never have materialized and our salvation would never have been accomplished. How deeply grateful we ought to be that the first round of the battle was so magnificently fought and so strategically won by our Lord in that desert place.

Jesus continued to deal with the enemy as he confronted him during his earthly ministry. He did this publicly—in spite of the alarm and panic this must have caused. It was not easy then—as it remains difficult now—to cope with the manifestation of demonic activity. Visible and verbal excess—physical shaking and screaming—seem to be evidences of the enemy's presence and unwillingness to be removed. I recognize that sometimes these manifestations can be evidences of the flesh rather than a demonstration by the demonic. However, the first response Jesus received to his ministry was surprise at the authority with which he taught (Mk 1:21-22) and recognition of who he was by the kingdom of darkness (Mk 1:23-24). It was regarded as 'new teaching' then (Mk 1:27) and two thousand years later, it continues to be regarded as 'new teaching'.

Undoubtedly Jesus left the disciples whom he called in no doubt about this particular area of their ministry and responsibility: 'You will have authority to drive out demons' (Mk 3:15; Lk 9:1; 10:17). Consequently, it is not surprising that when the church was born there was a recognition and awareness that this painful, unattractive and unwanted region of activity and ministry had to be tackled. Right from the beginning—before the church could begin to become what God intended it to be—Satan's power both inside as well as outside the church had to be recognized and crushed.

The incident of Ananias and Sapphira (Acts 5:1-11) raises serious intellectual and moral questions. Inevitably we ask, *how* did they die? What was the physical cause of their sudden death within such a short interval of each other? The question of *why* they died is even more difficult to cope with. Why should such an apparently small thing cause such drastic punishment? After all, in one way or another, all of us seem to be guilty of their kind of conduct in principle if not in detailed practice. They obviously wanted the others around them to think them what they were not. Obviously what we regard as small God will often regard as big, and conversely what we regard as big God will often regard as small. With our humanity, it is difficult for us to get God's perspective. Clearly, if hypocrisy were allowed to go unchecked the church would be wrecked. God took this sin seriously for that reason. This sin was to the new Israel (the church) what the sin of Achan had been to the old Israel (Josh 7). It led to a humiliating defeat of God's people, disdainful mocking by God's enemies, and God being given a bad name among the nations. The church has more to fear from corruption within than from opposition without. The fifth columnist is always a fearsome character—whatever guise he chooses to adopt. From this incident we need to recognize that Satan is the source (spotted and named through the use of a spiritual gift by Peter) and sin and death are the consequences. It does express a cautionary note to all of us—is there anything in my life which is damaging, endangering or crippling the church? We can either be a stone which Jesus will use to build his church (Mt 16:18) or a stone which has the potential of causing Jesus to stumble and struggle to build his church (Mt 16:23). Perhaps Peter recalled here (Acts 5:1-11) the bitter lesson which he had not yet learned before the event of Pentecost.

The immediate result of cleansing and purging inside the church—away from the prying investigation of a godless society—was devastating effectiveness by the church outside (Acts 5:12-16). Part of this very relevant public ministry was that 'those . . . who had evil spirits in them . . . were all healed'. This reality stands alongside the other evidences of God moving in power through his people. The ramparts of the kingdom of darkness are breached and the gates of hades are unable to resist the church's advance.

As the church continues to grow and its influence continues to be felt the battle with Satan's kingdom is frequently joined. 'There was great joy in that city' is Luke's observation in Samaria as the result of Philip's ministry (Acts 8:8). But it was not simply because of what he said—and that was dramatic enough to an audience which originally came from Jewish cultural roots—but it was also because of what the community saw. Part of that evidence was that 'evil spirits came out from many people with a loud cry . . .' Unnerving, unusual, hard to cope with theologically—but real.

The evidence was powerful enough to make Simon the magician want what he saw. He got his cheque book out to buy this trick for his act. He did not want to be upstaged, and so he wanted to buy what God wants to give freely. Again it took the operation of a spiritual gift by Peter to distinguish the bogus from the real. It does not appear that Simon ever did repent. He was much more concerned about his skin than he was about his sin (Acts 8:24). There is a strong tradition that he consistently opposed Peter and Paul for the rest of his days. However accurate or otherwise that legend may be, the Oxford English Dictionary defines simony as 'those who think they can buy something from God—particularly in church status'. Simony treats the church as if it were a kind of religious supermarket. Whatever the ultimate outcome, Satan will use the prominent as well as the private to create a thorn in the side of the new body of Christ on earth. Whether this appears inside or outside the church, it has to be painfully dealt with.

As Peter addresses the Gentiles under the commission of Christ, he raises an issue which continues to our own day: where do you draw the line between God's people and others? Some draw the line too narrowly—and need stretching, while others draw the line too broadly and need curtailing. The narrow ones allow God's favour to rest only on *their* group—defined by race, denomination or type, or whatever—while the broad ones give the impression that everyone is going to heaven somehow and sometime. God answers the dilemma by indicating that we must neither be too broad nor too narrow. Peter's background was Jewish exclusivism and he needed to be stretched. It is in this tension that he preaches the gospel to the Gentiles (Acts 10:34-43) with dramatic consequences (Acts 10:44-48). He declares that Jesus 'went everywhere, doing good and healing all who were under the power of the devil'. Jesus not only declared the word of the Father, but also did the works of the Father. Clearly not all illness is caused by demonic influence, but some is. Illness caused by a demonic influence affects most aspects of the human being—spiritual, mental, emotional, physical and social. The opposite is also true: the expulsion of the demonic presence or influence leads to the healing of all affected areas. Jesus demonstrated this ministry and Peter acknowledges it here to the Gentiles.

As the purposes of God continue to unfold, the course of evangelism moves from Antioch to Cyprus. This was the native heath and homeland of Barnabas. It is so easy to think that we will do better as Christian witnesses among people who do not know us and in a place that we do not know. However, a shrewd missionary once observed, 'When I got off the ship on a foreign shore the surroundings were different—but it was the same person who got on the ship.' Just so! Neither Saul of Tarsus nor Joseph named Barnabas ducked out of their responsibility to witness within the familiar setting and among their own folk. Saul went to Tarsus (Acts 11:25) and Barnabas went to Cyprus—the happy isle with its attractive climate and very fruitful industries. There they encountered demonic opposition in the form of Elymas the sorcerer (Acts 13:6-12). Roman governors normally had soothsayers to advise them. This, of course, is not an outdated practice—some delegates to the United Nations today retain their concern for and dependence on the occult. Political decisions are taken and strategic moves are made in a modern technological society in response to the question: 'Are the stars propitious?' In an article in *Time* magazine on the 17th June, 1972, the following comment was made:

> For all its trivial manifestations in tea-leaf readings and ritual gee-gaws, for all the outright nuts and charlatans it

attracts, occultism cannot be dismissed as mere fakery and faddishness. Clearly it is born of a religious impulse and in many cases becomes in effect a substitute faith.

At least one of our universities has a Chair for the occult.

Elymas in Paphos was a renegade Jew who knew the truth, and when the truth came to him he opposed it. He was concerned to block what God wanted to do. Saul of Tarsus confronted the demonic occult in him in a dramatic way—he made him blind. This was his first miracle! That is not normally what we look for in evangelism or in a church service! We normally conceive of miracles as healing and helping rather than hindering and harming. The Bible, however, is a powerful witness to the fact that miracles can do harm, as here. Saul is in no doubt about this man's pedigree:

> You son of the devil! You are the enemy of everything that is good. You are full of all kinds of evil tricks, and you always keep trying to turn the Lord's truths into lies! The Lord's hand will come down on you now; you will be blind and will not see the light of day for a time (Acts 13:10-11).

And it was so. Saul did to Elymas what Jesus had done to him on the Damascus road. This, however, was a powerful confrontation with the kingdom of darkness. Nine hundred years ago in Jarrow the Venerable Bede observed, 'The apostle, remembering his own case, knew that by the darkening of the eyes, the mind's darkness might be restored to light.'

So Elymas was deprived of his job—he could not tell fortunes any more while he was blind—and he was shut up literally and totally to God, presumably so that he could be delivered from the powerful hold that evil had on him. The direct result of this clear resistance to demonic powers was that the Cypriot governor was on his knees. 'When the governor saw what had happened, he believed; for he was greatly amazed at the teaching about the Lord' (Acts 13:12). Divine strategy normally gives sight as well as sound to the gospel—'one in the eye is worth two in the ear'. Evangelism and progress in the church are related to discerning and then dealing with demonic powers which oppose the work and the will of God.

So it is some time later when Paul sails for two days from Troas on the west side of what is now Turkey. Christianity was invading Europe. Conversion was the first lovely experience they had (Acts 16:15), but confrontation quickly followed (Acts 16:16-22)—and it happened on the way to a prayer meeting! The strength of the difficulty here was that what the fortune-teller was saying here was true—that 'these men are servants of the Most High God, who are telling you the way to be saved' (Acts 16:17). Often the devil's strategy is that he will give enough truth to impress us, but then he will control us, then cause disintegration in the personality and ultimately he will destroy the life.

Paul was obviously upset for two reasons. First of all, the manner in which she testified was disturbing. It is possible to say the right thing in the wrong way. We need constantly to remember that it is not just what we say that counts, but how we say it. The message can be accurate, but the manner in which we deliver it can be wrong. The fortune-teller's manner was an embarrassment—it was a discouragement to the gospel and preventing the truth getting through. It was closing minds rather than opening hearts. Secondly, Paul discerned that the source of her testimony was darkness rather than light. It is always necessary to be aware of where knowledge comes from, that is, from the flesh, the devil, or God. It is important to realize that the devil will not always feed you lies, he will sometimes feed you truth. In ministering deliverance to her Paul touched a very raw nerve in human nature—we are concerned sometimes to make money without regard to how we do it. This girl made fortunes by telling fortunes. Good news for the poor is often bad news for the rich. Deliverance for her meant deprivation for her handlers—and a riot resulted! (Acts 16:22)

Soon Paul was challenged to ministry in Athens (Acts 17:16-34)—that cultured and sophisticated city which was the birthplace of Socrates and Plato and the home of Aristotle. The Acropolis was the centre of religion there, dominated by the Parthenon and spawning many other temples and shrines. There were so many that people observed: 'If you go to Athens it is easier to meet a god than to meet a man.' In spite of this openness to religion, or maybe because of it (although some did become Christians in Athens), you never read of a church there. There is no letter to the Athenians as there are letters to the Corinthians and the Colossians and the Galatians and so on. Here was a community where the enemy had blinded the eyes of men and hardened the hearts of men to the truth. He had made the truth of God a lie, and men and women were held tightly in that grip and consequently unable to respond to the reality and joy of the gospel of Christ.

In what he must have regarded as his most effective ministry—at Ephesus—Paul was involved there too with the powers of darkness. The sons of Sciva (Acts 19:11-17) give us a baleful reminder of the danger of treating the demons with triviality. Doreen Irvine tells in her book, *From Witchcraft to Christ*—

> I yearned with all my heart to be pure, to be free, to love and serve Jesus Christ and him alone . . . I prayed and thanked the Lord Jesus for setting me free . . . But within a short time other demons revealed themselves to me. Some gave names, some didn't. I was in deep despair. I

> thought every demon had gone. Instead, some remained. I was very confused, but Mr Neil wasn't at all surprised. He knew that he had cast out just a few of all that had been within. A start had been made. The rest would go the same way as the first batch and to the same place. It couldn't all be done at once, at least not in my case. This is a powerful ministry, a deep and exhausting ministry. Sad to say, it is also a neglected one. My life had been an open door to demon-possession. It would be some time before I was completely free, before every demon would depart. Not that Jesus Christ could not have done it all at once and altogether. He could have. But as I have said before, his ways are past finding out . . . Mr Neil fasted and prayed before each session. He knew he was coming into contact with powers of darkness in an actual, genuine way. Therefore prayer and fasting are essential . . . Demons! Don't be silly, said the doctor. There are no such things as demons. It's all in your mind. You just need some treatment and then you'll be all right. So I was put to sleep for about ten days, and that was that . . . No-one believed demon-possession was real. No-one. There is no such person as the devil, let alone demons, I was told over and over again.[18]

Doreen Irvine goes on to tell of her awesome predicament which continued to torment her, and also of the commitment and godliness of the Baptist minister, the Rev Arthur Neil. She says of one night in Bristol, seven months after deliverance ministry had been exercised in the name of Jesus, according to Scripture, and in the power of the Holy Spirit —

> What a night of rejoicing that was! I was free. Jesus had done it. His mighty power was felt in a tremendous way by one and all. Mr Neil's face was aglow with the glory of God, and so was mine. Such praise went up in that church, such as was never heard before.It was truly a memorable night.

Luke recounts how dangerous it is to be involved with confronting the demonic carelessly and pretentiously—and yet as a result of the proper handling of demonic intrusion 'the name of the Lord Jesus was given greater honour' and 'in this powerful way the word of the Lord kept spreading and growing stronger'. Occult reality is neither to be ignored nor trivialized, but dealt with in the strong name of Jesus. This lies at the heart of the ongoing life and ministry of the early church—and we need to learn well from it.

Manifestations of demonic activity

Often the kingdom of darkness will manifest itself in ways which we have come to accept and live with. We justify these things in our own lives and in the lives of others and thereby deny the reality of the freedom to which Jesus calls us and by which Jesus' power is seen. Over the years we in our church have come to recognize many symptoms of enemy activity within us and among us:

Continuing compulsions

These certainly present a warning light. Not all compulsions are demonic, requiring deliverance in the name of Jesus. Some require healing or discipline rather than deliverance. But some compulsions will not yield to either healing or honest and faithful discipline and so do need deliverance. Smoking, drinking, overeating, talking, working, spending, interest in the occult are all compulsions which need to be acknowledged as potential symptoms which will yield only to godly deliverance if other measures prove unable to cope.

Chronic fear

This is another area which would indicate activity from

the power of darkness. Not all fear is wrong or destructive. Fear is a good servant, but a bad master—but it is not that kind of fear that I am referring to. Rather it is a paralysing, irrational fear which grips a person, rendering them helpless at certain times and in certain situations. God never intended us to remain in this kind of captivity.

Unnatural sexual desires

These betray demonic activity. Sex is God's gift to his creation, but what is intended to be good, creative and pure can become offensive, destructive and soiled. Sex is normally spoken of as 'making love' when in fact God intended that love should make sex. Some are dominated by sensual, lustful images and almost irresistible sexual demands which often lead to perverted expressions. God intends us to be free to respect, value and enjoy what he has given.

Involuntary feelings and desires

When these motivate completely irrational behaviour they betray enemy activity within. I remember someone coming to see me who confided at one point in the conversation, 'I was standing in a queue at the bank. Before I was attended to I just left and went out, got into my car, and drove and drove like a madman.' We saw her ministered to and delivered and returned to a peaceful, controlled and balanced way of life.

Weird or unbiblical beliefs

When these lead to strange and frequently immoral behaviour they are another symptom of satanic strategy. Doctrine is redefined and Scripture is interpreted in a strange and quite bizarre fashion and unusual behaviour results. The devil has always tampered with the word of God. If he cannot invalidate it, he will attempt to distort it.

An inordinate desire for attention

This ought also to alert us to a possible need for deliverance. This will display itself in the grossest sense of exhibitionism and dramatics. Sometimes this is what lies behind the attempted suicide.

The devil will sometimes cause *physical bondage,* as with the crippled woman (Lk 13:10-13). Though not all disease is demonic there is often a clear relationship between the two—especially where the physical symptoms cannot be understood or explained. It does require spiritual gifts to appreciate whether the need is for deliverance rather than healing.

Addictions

Addictions are normally a challenge to the power of Jesus by demonic powers—compulsive eating, dependence on alcohol, glue-sniffing, nicotine craving and drugs dependence are all features of this.

Intense, fierce hatred, bitterness, jealousy, rebellion and resentment

All of these open up territory which the enemy claims and possesses. He is fundamentally a legalist and claims what belongs to him by right. All of this territory is his, and we need to beware lest we give him ground for entry into our lives. He will certainly take immediate and lasting advantage unless we seek help to dislodge him.

Desire to remove ourselves from powerful Christian fellowship

This will accompany the other manifestations—especially where the ministry of deliverance is being offered. There is a clear logic in this.

We need to note carefully that it is not a sin to need deliverance, but it is sinful to need deliverance and yet not to want it. We have discovered that certain conditions need to be observed if deliverance is to be secured. The first of these is *humility* for we can either have our dignity or our deliverance, but seldom both. Secondly we need *honesty*. Hypocrisy and duplicity cannot remain if freedom is to be experienced. Thirdly we need to *confess* our sin—the importance of verbal confession must not be underplayed. Fourthly we need to *renounce* what is holding us captive for God will not count as an enemy what we regard as our friend. Fifthly *forgiveness* of all others is required. We have noted frequently that the devil's two favourite loopholes by which he will gain entry are involvement in some form of occult practice and preserving unforgiveness in our hearts. Finally we need to *call* on the name of the Lord. There is only one deliverer—Jesus Christ—and deliverance will only come in his name by the power of the Holy Spirit.

Within our own church and ministry here we use the following prayer as a guide and help as we encourage people to come into freedom in Christ:

> Almighty God, I renounce in the name of Jesus what you have shown this day to be a demonic stronghold in my life—and I receive your deliverance by the power of your Holy Spirit and will live in freedom there with the freedom with which Jesus has set me free.
>
> Father, I forgive. I lay down my bitterness, my resentment, my hatred, rebellion. I thank you, God, that I am accepted in Christ. I am a child of God. Heaven is my home. I belong to the best family in the universe. There is royal blood in my veins.
>
> Lord Jesus Christ, I believe you are the Son of God and the only way to God. You died on the cross for my sins, and you rose again from the dead. I repent of all my sins,

and I forgive every other person, as I would have God forgive me; all those who have rejected me and hurt me and failed to show me love. God, I forgive them all now. I trust you for your forgiveness, and I believe, Lord, that you accept me right now as I am in Christ. I am accepted; I am the object of your special care; you really love me; you want me. You are my Father.

Lord, I want to thank you. And I want to tell you one more thing; I accept myself in Christ in the way you made me. I am your workmanship. I thank you for what you've done, and I believe you will go on working in me until you complete what you have begun.

And so, Lord, release me from any dark, evil pressure, I release my spirit to rejoice in you as your Holy Spirit would enable me. In Jesus' name. Amen.

10

The End of the Beginning

Inherent in the whole climate of the Acts of the Apostles is a very powerful consolation and motivation—that Jesus will return to this planet just as surely as the apostles had seen him go from it. They realized in a powerful and unforgettable way that they were living between the two greatest events in history—the first coming of Christ and the second coming. Even if the latter is delayed it can no more be denied than the reality of the first advent.

There are two occasions in world history when someone from outside our world comes inside—one has already occurred and the other has yet to happen. Jesus never said, 'I was born'—he always referred to his coming to earth in the first place as 'I came' (Mt 20:28; Mk 10:45; Lk 7:34; 19:10; Jn 3:19). That is an unusual way to speak of birth. When Jesus eventually confronted and challenged the disciples about his true nature (Mt 16:13-16) he was told that society generally concluded that he was a reincarnation of John the Baptist or Elijah or Jeremiah or some other prophet. They judged that someone with his authority and experience could not have become so in thirty short years. Peter, however, was the spokesman who verbalized his true nature with all the pent-up pathos of a Jew whose ancestors had been waiting for the fulfilment of the promised Messiah for a thousand years—'You are the Messiah, the Son of the living God.' In other words, 'You are not a reincarnation—whatever men may say —you are an incarnation. You did not have a previous existence on earth, but you did have a previous existence in heaven!'

Such is the watershed of the gospels. The fulcrum of Acts, however, is that after Jesus ascended to heaven and left them, the apostles anticipated his return, and until that time his Holy Spirit would equip and enable them for all the challenges and changes that were to be part of their (and our) experience. Unforgettable to them were his transforming words, 'Do not leave Jerusalem, but wait for the gift I told you about, the gift my Father promised. John baptized with water, but in a few days you will be baptized with the Holy Spirit.' Equally unforgettable was the overwhelming drama of his ascension and the powerful assurance from the two messengers of God: 'Galileans, why are you standing there looking up at the sky? This Jesus who was taken from you into heaven, will come back in the same way that you saw him go to heaven.' They communicated this assurance to a bewildered and wondering populace, mutely asking how it was that a forty-year-old cripple could be so completely restored and energized (Acts 3:20-21).

When Jesus was born, it was in the little unspectacular township of Bethlehem. When he finally left his disciples, his point of departure was just over seven miles down the road from the Mount of Olives. When he returns it will be to that mountain. So far as geography is concerned Jesus travelled little, yet the world will never be the same again. Persecution, pain, misunderstanding, injustice, loneliness, mockery and brutal death were all part of the early church's lot, but always they held on to this one reality—Jesus will come back to reign!

Colin Morris insists in *The Hammer of the Lord* that you cannot go 'back' to God. God is always up front, calling us forward, not back to the good old days. The hope of Christ's return is not a doctrine or a dogma to be bounced around in a discussion group or for us to pass an opinion on it; it is a fact to change our lives and to have a fundamental bearing on our attitude to life. Whenever the Bible speaks about Christ's second coming its purpose is always to challenge us to action. When the biblical writers refer to it, their purpose is not to give a detailed explanation of the doctrine, but to relate it to practical needs. When we really see how this hope is meant to affect our lives, we can never be the same again. We are living now 'between the times'—between the time when Jesus introduced God's new era and the time when he will return to establish God's kingdom in its final form. This is not a time for our suppositions or our pre-conceived prejudices, when we sit around in our spiritual ghettos killing time as if we were waiting for a train that is not on time according to our personally devised timetable. It is a time for action, a time for distinctive Christian living.

We know *how* Jesus will come—in maturity and not as a baby; in glory and not in humility and poverty; in plain, unmistakable public view and not in hard-to-find obscurity. We know *where* Jesus will come—his feet will touch the Mount of Olives first of all. We know *what* will happen when he comes—the dead will rise from the elements where their bodies have rested; those Christians who remain on earth alive will join them without ever tasting the experience of death; both will meet together with Jesus in the air (presumably because there is nowhere on earth big enough to contain such a large, rejoicing, resurrected company); all will be able to look down on Jerusalem and Galilee and look around at every country and corner of the earth represented in that transformed company of redeemed men and women—and yet to have eyes for only one person—our Lord and Saviour Jesus Christ.

However, no one knows *when* he will come. Jesus, on earth, clearly had an understanding of God's programme, but not this part! It is foolish and filled with frustration to speculate about the time, and even more foolhardy to stipulate exactly when this will occur. Melody Green, wife of the late Keith Green, whose music has stimulated and blessed so many of us, sums up the main thrust of Acts in the refrain of one of her songs:

> Thank you, oh my Father, for giving us your Son,
> And leaving your Spirit till
> The work on earth is done.[19]

When the perfect Jesus comes, then all the imperfect with which we have struggled for so long will disappear. It is to this next great event in history, this great divine far-off event to which the whole of creation moves, that we all look forward and anticipate with an unlimited hope. The three things which each of us needs, and the three virtues of the Christian life, are faith, hope, and love. Faith is the essence of the Christian gospel, since it is willing to accept what it cannot understand and so finds its chief occupation is obtaining the promises of God. Love is the greatest of these three, since it is fundamental to transforming and sustaining real relationships both with God and with man. But hope is the most neglected of them. This is the age of despair. It is true that every passing generation has produced its crop of Hamlets, morbidly introvertive, hypersensitive, over-wrought, contemplating suicide and crying:

> The time is out of joint. O cursed spite,
> That ever I was born to set it right.

This has probably always been so, but it is much more prevalent today than ever before.

Two days before Albert Einstein died in 1955, he and Bertrand Russell delivered their Manifesto in London in which they said, 'We have found that the men who know the most are the most gloomy.' 'Mankind,' writes Lewis Mumford, 'is afloat on a frail life-raft.' If more people are afraid today, it is because they possess the apparatus of fear to a greater degree than ever before. If more people are corroded with guilt, it is because conscience has been tampered with more effectively than at any other time. If more people are plagued by a sense of blank meaninglessness, it is because fewer meanings have been left unmolested. Anxiety and despair have invaded our lives, not only on an individual level, but on a political and social level.

Arthur Koestler, who along with his wife recently expressed the ultimate despair by committing suicide, described how he felt in his autobiographical *Arrow in the Blue*:

> This latent apprehension, the awareness of guilt and impending punishment, seemed to be always present, like the rhythmic beat of the surf at night along the shore. While there are voices under the open window and laughter on the pier one is able to forget it, but when the laughter dies away and voices are stilled, the muffled thunder swells up again and one realises that it has always been present, and that the waves will never stop beating their heads against the stones of the pier.[20]

All around us the absence of realistic, resilient hope

is emphasized by the presence of substitutes: a bland, unthinking optimism; a disturbing, corrosive escapism, so often taking the route of violence, drugs and noise; a frenetic, abandoned trip of self-indulgence; a mystical, naive pursuit of astrology; a penetrating, clinical and radical idealism that will not take account of the facts of the matter. Then there is an almost insatiable yearning for the past that romanticizes what were often dismal and difficult years. This motivates thousands who want to participate in the BBC's programme *The Good Old Days* and enables the late Laura Ashley to build a commercial empire on fabrics of the past. Alvin Toffler calls this 'the psychological lust for the simpler, less turbulent past'.[21] Others practise an uncertain groping in the dark, hoping against hope, and search for inner peace and security as they contemplate Zen Buddhism, listen to Hindu gurus or in desperation turn to the ouija board or black magic rites. These are some of the 'philosophies' of life which are being embraced today—and all demonstrate vividly that man cannot live without hope.

We need a hope which takes seriously the nature of man himself. Acts breathes hope in the midst of all the suffering and sadness, as man copes with all the disappointment and despair that exists within him and around him—inside as well as outside the church. These ordinary men and women were committed to the conclusion that God had acted in Jesus Christ crucified, risen and exalted—and one day he would return to reign. For them—and indeed for us—Jesus is the key to hope.

They mirrored a dominating note which is struck again and again in the New Testament period. One out of every thirty verses in Scripture mentions this hope (1,200 times in the Old Testament and over 300 times in the New Testament). There are about the same number of references to the return of Jesus in the New Testament as there are references to the cross. Significantly, for every mention of the first advent of Christ—Christmas—there are eight mentions of his second advent. In the 216 chapters of the New Testament there are 318 references to it. Whole books of the New Testament (1 and 2 Thess, for example) and whole chapters (Mt 24; Mk 13; Lk 21) are devoted to it. It is the theme of the prophets of the Old Testament: 'It was concerning this salvation that the prophets made careful search and investigation, and they prophesied about this gift which God would give you. They tried to find out when the time would be and how it would come. This was the time to which Christ's Spirit was pointing, in predicting the sufferings that Christ would have to endure and the glory that would follow (1 Pet 1:10-11).

The angels bore witness to the first advent as they intruded unexpectedly into the pastoral nightshift of the shepherds on duty in Bethlehem's fields and dramatically declared: 'Don't be afraid! I am here with good news for you, which will bring great joy to all the people. This very day in David's town your Saviour was born—Christ the Lord! And this is what will prove it to you—you will find a baby wrapped in strips of cloth and lying in a manger' (Lk 2:10-12). Suddenly the lone messenger of God was joined by 'a great army of heaven's angels . . . singing praises to God: "Glory to God in the highest heaven, and peace on earth to those with whom he is pleased!"' The angels also bore witness to the second advent with equal suddenness when the apostles were startled by Jesus' ascension: 'Galileans, why are you standing there looking up at the sky? This Jesus, who was taken from you into heaven, will come back in the same way that you saw him go to heaven' (Acts 1:10-11). Twenty-three of the twenty-seven New Testament books contain references to the return of Christ.

Only four (Galatians, which was written for a special purpose; Philemon, 2 and 3 John, which are significantly short letters) have no reference to the second coming. When you compare all this mass of biblical evidence with the fact that the Lord's Supper is mentioned only seven times—it is startling that many would be unwilling to neglect communion, and yet they never think of nor adjust their lives to the reality of the return of Christ.

Lord Shaftesbury, who could never be charged with sitting in isolated, cloistered cosiness removed from the pains and pressures of his society, said towards the end of his life, 'I do not think that in the last forty years I have lived one conscious hour that was not influenced by the thought of our Lord's return.'[22] Such was also the climate of the New Testament and the atmosphere which pervaded the church in Acts constantly. The return of Christ provided not a doctrine to be debated and discussed, but a fact against which the whole of life was to be lived and the purposes of God were to be appreciated and carried out. Professor Swete says succinctly in his commentary, 'The tone of the prediction is wholly practical.' Having lost its significance, as well as an awareness of its reality, we need to recapture it and live our lives and serve God's purposes in the light of it.

The personal character of the return of Jesus is shown by the Greek word most frequently used for it—the *parousia.* In ordinary, secular Greek this was the word used for the visit of the emperor or other distinguished person. A literal translation would be 'being nearby', so that it contains the two ideas of 'approach' and 'presence', with a suggestion of honour due to the person to whom it refers. It is well illustrated in 2 Corinthians 7:6-7, where the apostle Paul describes the pleasure which the advent or 'coming' of Titus gave him: 'But God, who encourages the downhearted, encouraged us with the coming [*parousia*] of Titus. It was not only his coming [*parousia*] that cheered us, but also his report of how you encouraged him . . . and so I am even happier now.' The lonely, forsaken Paul looked forward to the warmth and genuineness of Titus' company, but also because of the implications of his coming to him. The same thought is present when he writes of the 'coming' of Stephanas, Fortunatus and Achaicus (1 Cor 16:17), or his own 'coming' to Philippi (Phil 1:26). Both these events are happy and affect the present in the light of the future.

Referring to the 'coming' of Jesus Christ, *parousia* is used seven times by Paul, four times by Matthew, three times by Peter, twice by James, and once by John. In every case it clearly was a word in common use to indicate the actual, literal, visible coming of a person or group of persons. In the second century it was used in isolation to mean the second coming of Jesus Christ.

Another word, *epiphaneia,* used only by Paul, has a more general character, and means 'appearing'. In his letter to the Christians at Thessalonica (2 Thess 2:8) it is accompanied with the overwhelming of Christ's dazzling presence. Paul also uses *epiphaneia* to speak of the first coming of Christ into the world. *Epiphaneia* not only has this substantial, historical ring about it, but conveys the idea of meeting once again with someone who is already known.

The return of Jesus is also described as the 'revelation'—*apokalupsis*—of Jesus Christ. These references indicate that it is an event in the future. 'He will appear a second time,' says the writer to the Hebrews, 'not to deal with sin, but to save those who are waiting for him' (Heb 9:28). Taking all these words together we get a very clear picture of the return of our Lord Jesus Christ as it is seen through the faithful, hopeful eyes of the early church. It would mean his presence after his absence, the shining out of his glory after his awesome humiliation, and the unveiling of his power and majesty. Taken together they indicate that the return of Jesus will be an unquestioned historical event—real, tangible and powerfully recognizable.

Undoubtedly this was the attitude of the early church —they looked back with deep thanksgiving to the cross where he dealt with our sins; they looked up to the heavens where he is seated on the right hand of God the Father Almighty, constantly interceding on our behalf; but they also looked forward to his coming again—and so should we if we are to get our present life and service into perspective. According to the New Testament that return is an event, not a process; and it is personal and bodily in form. It is this event which God intends should have a profoundly practical effect upon the lives that we live within society.

Long before feminism became an offensive feature, with all kinds of unhappy implications, Christabel Pankhurst took vigorous action to challenge our society to a biblical understanding of women. She could never be described as a withdrawn citizen of the United Kingdom unrelated to reality. She became deeply involved in the campaign for votes for women. In her book *The Lord Cometh* she writes, 'By what seemed a chance discovery in a bookshop, I came across writings on prophecy which pointed out that in the Bible there are oracles foretelling and diagnosing the world's ills, and promising that they should be cured.' This was to be brought about, not by political agitation, but by the Lord's return. 'It seemed too good to be true,' she writes. This changed the course of her life radically, and this brilliant young law student gave herself up to lecturing in public on the return of Christ as foretold in the Scriptures. While the return of Jesus Christ to earth—personal and visible—is by no means free from controversy, the fact remains that where it has been taken seriously—as in the New Testament—it has a significant practical bearing upon the Christian life. It is also intensely personal, and whether the writer is Paul, Peter, John, or Luke, as in the Acts of the Apostles, he is looking forward with intense desire to the time when he himself shall see his Lord and Saviour face to face.

There is one more expression, frequently misunderstood, which must still be looked at. At the end of Paul's first letter to the Corinthians, after sending greetings to his friends and adding his signature, he says, 'Whoever does not love the Lord—a curse on him! Our Lord, come!' The original text gives three words to end 1 Corinthians 16:22 *'anathema. Marana tha.' Anathema* is a Greek word meaning 'set aside' or 'put away', often for a special use, such as a votive offering. However, *Marana tha* are two Aramaic words meaning 'Our Lord, come!' Their introduction without any explanation into a letter written in Greek shows that they were in current use, and would be immediately understood by Paul's readers, many of whom were Gentiles in origin and not Jewish. That this is actually the case is confirmed by the fact that the two words, *Marana tha,* appear in early Christian writings such as the *Didache* as a form of thanksgiving to be used after the Lord's Supper. It appears to have been a very common greeting within Christian fellowship in the early church. Paul uses a Greek equivalent in his letter to the Christians in the first Christian bridgehead in Europe at Philippi. He says to them as he issues his final practical instructions, 'Show a gentle attitude towards everyone. The Lord is coming soon' (Phil 4:5). This explains 1 Corinthians 16:22, where Paul appears to be saying, as a closing forceful statement, 'The Lord is coming. Do you love him in a practical and obvious way? If you don't, then the Christian fellowship is no place for you and you need to be set apart and separated from it.'

Among all that is hard to understand in the prophecies of the Bible the promise of the Lord's return stands out clear and certain. It is simply and clearly declared by Jesus himself and affirmed again and again by Peter and John. It is a recurring theme of Paul, whom God used to write half the New Testament. Quite obviously it is important for us, as it was undoubtedly fundamental to the understanding and response of the Acts church, that we should understand the bearing of the fact of the Lord's return upon our own lives, even though in the contemporary church it has been largely the preserve of the fanatical. We need to lay aside the doubts and difficulties—and they are not inconsiderable—and allow the fact of the Second Coming of Christ to have a direct bearing upon our thinking and living.

An artist has depicted a young woman standing on a cliff, looking out to sea, her hand shading her eyes, as she scans the horizon for the first sign of her husband's returning ship. The artist's expertise clearly conveys her expectation and intense desire. It is because she believes her husband's word about the time of his return that her eagerness dominates the picture. She loves him and his presence means more to her than anything else in the world. For this reason she will recall exactly what he said when he promised to return, and especially what he told her about the time when she might expect to see him. She will look for some sign of his ship; she will prepare for him the welcome that is always ready in her heart.

Perhaps you may judge this picture to be a little quaint, and yet it cuts through the veneer of sophistication which often robs our contemporaries of the joys of life, and it also portrays something of the attitude which should characterize our awaiting the return of our Lord Jesus. It is for this reason that we will want to study every word of promise held firm in Scripture and scan the political horizon for any sign that the time of its fulfilment is drawing near—whether it is the evidence of unprecedented violence throughout the world, the escalating and frightening moral decline within and among the nations, the political manoeuvering leading towards some form of global unification under a world dictator, or even the restoration of the Jews to their own land with all the political and moral confusion that that has created. The Bible tells us enough about the return of Christ to stimulate and strengthen faith, even if it does not satisfy our curiosity.

> O Lord, 'tis for Thee, for Thy coming, we wait;
> The sky, not the grave, is our goal;
> O, trump of the angel! O, voice of the Lord!
> Blessed hope! Blessed rest of my soul!

Such was the climate of hope and expectancy which permeated the early church and influenced its attitudes and activities. So must it be for us as we look to the past for a future.

Notes

1. J. B. Phillips, *The Young Church in Action* (Geoffrey Bles), Translator's Preface, p.vii.
2. S. C. Neill, *Christian Faith Today* (Penguin, 1955).
3. Quoted in David Watson, *I Believe in the Church* (Hodder & Stoughton, 1982) pp.15-16.
4. Andrew Woolsey, biography of Duncan Campbell (Hodder & Stoughton) p.177.
5. Frank Laubach, quoted in Arnold Bittlinger, *Gifts and Graces* (Hodder & Stoughton) p.56.
6. Arnold Bittlinger, *Gifts and Graces* (Hodder & Stoughton) p.81.
7. Quoted in David Watson, *I Believe in the Church* (Hodder & Stoughton, 1982) p.103.
8. Juan Carlos Ortiz, *Call to Discipleship* (Logos International, New Jersey, and Good Reading Ltd, London) pp.42-43.
9. Quoted in William Barclay, *Ambassador for Christ* (St Andrew Press, 1973) p.12.
10. *John Wesley's Journal* (James Askew & Sons) p.43.
11. Dr J. Packer, *Under God's Word* (Marshall Pickering, 1980) p.41.
12. *Open Doors* magazine (Open Doors, 1985).

13. Quoted by David Watson, *I Believe in Evangelism* (Hodder & Stoughton, 1979) p.37.
14. *John Wesley's Journal* (James Askew & Sons) p.59.
15. J. S. Stewart, *Teach Yourself Preaching* p.37.
16. Dietrich Bonhoeffer, *The Cost of Discipleship* (SCM Press, 1964) pp.35-37.
17. Quoted by William Barclay, *The Promise of the Spirit* (Epworth Press, 1960) p.47.
18. Doreen Irvine, *From Witchcraft to Christ* (Concordia Press, 1973) pp.125,137.
19. M. Green © Birdwing/Word Music (UK), 1982.
20. Quoted by Murdo Ewen Macdonald, *The Need to Believe* (Collins [Fontana], 1959) p.10.
21. Quoted by Stephen Travis, *The Jesus Hope* (Word [UK], 1974) p.17.
22. Quoted by G. T. Manley, *The Return of Jesus Christ* (IVP, 1960) p.20.

Joy Unspeakable

by D. Martyn Lloyd-Jones

What does it mean to be baptized with the Holy Spirit?

Can I be a Christian and still not baptized with the Spirit?

What difference will the baptism with the Spirit make in my Christian life?

Straightforward, powerful and with disarming candour, Doctor Lloyd-Jones expounds the Scriptures on an issue that has both united and sadly divided Christians everywhere. Drawing on the experiences of great men of God in years gone by, he challenges us to examine the Scriptures without prejudice, and encourages us to seek the Lord for all the blessing and equipping that he is pleased to give.

Kingsway Publications

The Father Heart of God

by Floyd McClung

What is God like?

Has he got time for twentieth-century men and women?

Does he really care?

In his work with *Youth with a Mission*, Floyd McClung has met many who suffer from deep emotional hurts and fears.

Time and again it has been the discovery of God as Father—perfect and reliable, unlike any human parent—that has brought healing and liberty.

This book is for you . . .

. . . if you find it hard to accept God as a loving father, or
. . . if you know God's love but would like to share his blessing with others more effectively.

Kingsway Publications

Renewal Down to Earth

by Robert L. Roxburgh

'I want to share the experience and insights which God has given me in my own pilgrimage — to help the many ordinary, local churches that seek a more vital life but have not as yet moved very far along the way.'

Some books on renewal inspire us with their ideals but leave us feeling that the writer lives far from practical, down-to-earth realities. But God is very much concerned with what will *work* in real-life situations. This book reflects that belief. Bob Roxburgh's experience and understanding of Scripture combine to show that renewal can come even where a church appears almost lifeless, as long as its members are open to the direction of the Holy Spirit and ready to count the cost of change.

After twenty-five years in North America, BOB ROXBURGH returned to Britain to become Senior Pastor of the Millmead Centre (Guildford Baptist Church). He is married with three children.

Kingsway Publications